JN081347

宮沢賢治
原文英訳シリーズ1

『銀河鉄道の夜』を英語で読む

収録作品
『銀河鉄道の夜』
『インドラの網』
『マグノリアの木』
『春と修羅』序

コスモピア

はじめに

森羅万象の中の小さな要素

　宮沢賢治（1896-1933）は明治時代後期の1896年8月、日本が日清戦争に勝利した1年ほど後に生まれ、昭和初期、1933年に亡くなりました。

　日清戦争（1894－1895）は、日本が近代になって初めて経験した大きな戦争であり、日本が世界の大国としての地位を確立するきっかけとなった戦争でもありました。そして賢治が亡くなったのは、1933年9月、日本が中国への侵略を「正当化」するために起こした1931年の満州事変から、ほぼ2年後のことです。

　賢治が生きた時代は、平安時代（794-1185）以来、日本の歴史の中でも最も急速に発展、激動し、そして劇的に変化した時代でした。大日本帝国が発展し、日本人の間に国民性の意味と意義が新たに認識された時代でもありました。

　岩手県の花巻という小さな町の出身である賢治は、この日本の発展に驚きを感じ、感嘆を覚えていました。子どもから大人になりつつあった頃、この近代的な世界に出会い、その発展のさまをただ傍観しているだけではなく、完全に吸収しようとしました。地質学、天文学、農学の勉強、木版画の収集、チェロやハルモニウムの演奏、作曲、タイプライターの習得などを、執拗なまでの熱意と奔放な情熱で行ったのです。

　日本人が世界における自分たちのアイデンティティや、アジアや遠く離れた場所での自分たちの位置づけに執着していた時代、賢治は自分の

国の人々とはまったくかけ離れた存在でした。彼の物語や詩の中には、日本や日本人についての言及はほとんどありません。同胞が高らかに叫んでいた大日本帝国や日本人の民族としてのアイデンティティの問題にも賢治の関心は向きませんでした。当時の編集者や読者が彼を無視したのも無理はありません。彼の深い関心事は、当時の日本人や世界の人々の関心事とはまったく異なっていたのですから。

　宮沢賢治にとって人間としてのアイデンティティとは、ナショナリズムとかエスニシティの枠組みではなく、すべての創造物、あるいは森羅万象の中の小さな要素にしか過ぎないものとしての位置づけの中で定義されていました。

　私は1970年に『銀河鉄道の夜』の英語版の初翻訳を終えて、それを日本文学の翻訳出版で有名な出版社に持ち込みました。しかしその出版社の編集の責任者から「宮沢賢治は日本を代表する作家ではない」と言われて出版を断られました。

　当時、谷崎潤一郎（1886-1965）は亡くなってまだ5年、三島由紀夫（1925-1970）はまだ存命中で、川端康成（1899-1972）はわずか2年前にノーベル文学賞を受賞していました。この3人の作家の作品は、それぞれ大きく異なる特徴もありますが、日本人の感性、文化のさまざまなニュアンスを「代表」する作家であったことには間違いありません。

　しかし宮沢賢治の目は、星に向けられていたのでした。

2023年4月
ロジャー・パルバース
Roger Pulvers

目次

『銀河鉄道の夜』
Night on the Milky Way Train

読むまえに――
宮沢賢治―― 21世紀宇宙の旅
気がつくと、列車に乗って銀河を旅するジョバンニと親友のカンパネルラ。その不思議な旅と出会いは何のメタファーなのか。

『インドラの網』
Indra's Net

読むまえに――
天の空間を感じとる
宇宙のあらゆるものを繋いでいるという「インドラの網」。その向こうに広がる空間と光景を想像しながら、この美しい小品を味わってみよう。

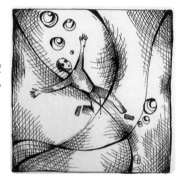

イラスト：ルーシー・バルバース

本書の宮沢賢治の原作は「宮沢賢治全集」（ちくま文庫）を底本としています。

その上で、『銀河鉄道の夜』『インドラの網』『マグノリアの木』の3編については新仮名遣いに変更するとともに一部の漢字を改めています。

韻文である「『春と修羅』序」に関しては、底本のまま旧仮名遣いで掲載しています。

音声ダウンロードの方法

音声をスマートフォンや PC で、簡単に
聞くことができます。

方法1 スマホで聞く場合

面倒な手続きなしにストリーミング再生で聞くことができます。

※ストリーミング再生になりますので、通信制限などにご注意ください。
また、インターネット環境がない状況でのオフライン再生はできません。

このサイトにアクセスするだけ！

https://soundcloud.com/yqgfmv3ztp15/
sets/4qxo5bicbni3

❶
上記サイトにアクセス！

❷ アプリを使う場合は
SoundCloud に
アカウント登録 (無料)

方法2 パソコンで音声ダウンロードする場合

パソコンで mp3 音声をダウンロードして、スマホなどに取り込むこと
も可能です。

(スマホなどへの取り込み方法はデバイスによって異なります)

❶ 下記のサイトにアクセス

https://www.cosmopier.com/
download/4864541961

❷ 中央のボタンをクリックする

音声は PC の一括ダウンロード用圧縮ファイル (ZIP 形式) でご提供します。
解凍してお使いください。

音声ファイル表

タイトルと本文は同じ音声ファイルの中に収録されています。そのため、4つの作品ではタイトルページが示されています。

電子版の使い方

音声ダウンロード不要
ワンクリックで音声再生！

本書購読者は
無料でご使用いただけます！
音声付きで
本書がそのままスマホでも
読めます。

電子版ダウンロードには
クーポンコードが必要です

詳しい手順は下記をご覧ください。
右下の QR コードからもアクセスが
可能です。

電子版：無料引き換えコード
G8t3Rg

ブラウザベース（HTML5 形式）でご利用
いただけます。

★クラウドサーカス社 ActiBook電子書籍
（音声付き）です。

●対応機種
・PC (Windows/Mac)　・iOS (iPhone/iPad)
・Android（タブレット、スマートフォン）

電子版ご利用の手順

❶コスモピア・オンラインショップにアクセス
してください。（無料ですが、会員登録が必要です）
https://www.cosmopier.net/

❷ログイン後、カテゴリ「電子版」のサブカテゴリ「書籍」をクリックして
ください。

❸本書のタイトルをクリックし、「カートに入れる」をクリックしてください。

❹「カートへ進む」→「レジに進む」と進み、「クーポンを変更する」をクリック。

❺「クーポン」欄に本ページにある無料引き換えコードを入力し、「登録する」を
クリックしてください。

❻0 円になったのを確認して、「注文する」をクリックしてください。

❼ご注文を完了すると、「マイページ」に電子書籍が登録されます。

宮沢賢治　略年譜

1896年〈明治29年〉8月、岩手県現在の花巻市に生まれる

1909年（明治42年）4月、岩手県立盛岡中学校に入学

1914年（大正3年）3月、盛岡中学校卒業

1915年（大正4年）4月、盛岡高等農林学校入学

1917年（大正6年）7月、同人誌『アザリア』を発行

1918年（大正7年）3月、農林学校を卒業。研究生として残る

1920年（大正9年）5月、農林学校研究生を卒業。10月、法華宗系在家仏教団体、国柱会に入信

1921年（大正10年）東京に出奔するも地元に戻り、10月、稗貫郡立稗貫農学校（翌年、花巻農学校に）の教諭に

1922年（大正11年）11月27日、妹のトシ死去。『永訣の朝』

1923年（大正12年）『マグノリアの木』

1924年（大正13年）『春と修羅』を自費出版。『銀河鉄道の夜』に着手。

1926年（大正15年）3月、花巻農学校を依願退職。その後も農業指導などに関わる

1928年（昭和3年）肺浸潤の診断をうける。その後、一時回復するも病臥生活に

1929年（昭和4年）『インドラの網』

1931年（昭和6年）『雨ニモマケズ』

1933年〈昭和8年〉9月21日、死去

1934年（昭和9年）死後『銀河鉄道の夜』出版

銀河鉄道の夜
Night on the Milky Way Train

イラスト：ルーシー・パルパース

Night on the Milky Way Train を読むまえに

宮沢賢治—21世紀宇宙の旅

銀河を旅する列車の中で、ジョバンニと親友のカンパネルラは、不思議な光景と人々に出会う。ふたりはなぜこの列車に乗っているのか、そしてこの列車は、一体どこへ向かおうとしているのだろうか？

　宮沢賢治が『銀河鉄道の夜』を書き始めたのは1924年のことです。この小説の発想と、完成させるための力を賢治にもたらした出来事が、その2年ほど前、正確には1922年11月27日に起きたことは明らかです。その日、最愛の妹、トシが24歳で亡くなったのです。宇宙をめぐる銀河鉄道の旅は、賢治がその詩「永訣の朝」の冒頭2行で、

**けふのうちに
とほくへいつてしまふわたくしのいもうとよ**

と描いたトシの旅に同行するものでした。

　賢治は少なくとも1924年から7年間、この小説に取り組み、原稿を残しました。賢治が亡くなった翌年の1934年、高村光太郎らが編集した文圃堂書店版で初めてこの『銀河鉄道の夜』は出版されたのです。以来、日本では英語が原作の『不思議の国のアリス』や『たのしい川べ』と並び称される日本最大の児童文学作品のひとつになりました。

　『銀河鉄道の夜』のストーリーはシンプルです。

　ジョバンニと親友のカンパネルラのふたりはいつの間にか、宇宙を走る列車に乗っています。この列車の旅で、ふたりはさまざまな奇妙でそして素晴らしい人びとに出会います。そして、天の川のほとりでめくるめく光景を目にし、さまざまな不思議な出来事に遭遇します。

　しばらくすると、車掌が現れ、切符を見せるように言います。ジョバンニがポケットに手を入れると、偶然にもポケットの中に折り畳まれた緑色の切符がありました。それを取り出して見せると、車掌も乗客も驚嘆します。ジョバンニが取り出した切符は、時空を超えてどこまでも行ける切符だったのです。実は、この小説の中で「ジョバンニの切符」と題された章は、圧倒的に長く、最も重要な章なのでしょう。

ジョバンニの切符は想像上のフリーパスであり、賢治の妹のトシと一緒にあの世へ、この世よりずっとよい世界へ旅立つ自分を、想像したかったのでしょう。

　しかし、ジョバンニが「どこまでも一緒に行ける」と確信していたにもかかわらず、カンパネルラはあっという間に姿を消してしまいます。カンパネルラは、南十字星の脇にある、大きな暗黒星雲である真っ暗な「石炭袋」(そらの孔)の中に消えてしまったのです。

　ジョバンニは目覚めると、丘の上にいました。川へ駆け下りると、ひとりの少年が溺れているのを知るのです。少年はカンパネルラで、川に落ちた別の少年を助けようとしたのです。いじめっ子だった別の少年の命は救われましたが、その少年を助けたカンパネルラは川の底に消えてしまいます。

　1970年にこの小説の翻訳に着手して以来、私は4回のリライトを繰り返しました。1983年9月から *The Mainichi Daily News* 新聞*に週1回の連載で『銀河鉄道の夜』の英訳 *Night on the Milky Way Train* を掲載しました。『銀河鉄道の夜』の英訳版が登場したのはこのときが初めてでした。

　賢治の散文や詩を翻訳する場合、彼の叙情的で独特な文体を英語で再現することが課題のひとつになります。しかし、幸いなことに日本語と同様に豊かで多様なオノマトペの宝庫である英語の中からは、賢治の文に対応する英語のオノマトペを掘り起こすことができました。1967年に賢治の文学を読み始めたとき、私は賢治のユニークなオノマトペの使い方に魅了され、彼を「ミヤザワザワ賢治」と呼ぶようにしたぐらいです。

　銀河ステーションへの到着が告げられたとき、ジョバンニが目にした見事な光景で見られるように、賢治は光の描写に最も強い叙情性を発揮

　*現在は *The Mainichi*　https://mainichi.jp/english/

しているかもしれません。 海からの光「まるで億万の蛍烏賊の火を一ぺんに化石させて、そら中に沈めた」と、空からの光「かくして置いた金剛石を、誰かがいきなりひっくりかえして、ばら撒いた」（p.44 ～ 45参照）の融合は、自然の中のあらゆるものを一度に観察し、体験することができる賢治の能力の象徴です。だから私は宮沢賢治を「光の詩人」と呼ぶわけです。

　カンパネルラが「石炭袋」の中に消えていく直前、ジョバンニは、「ほんとうのさいわいは一体何だろう」という問いをカンパネルラに投げかけます。その問いは賢治にとっても最も重要な問いでした。それに対してカンパネルラは「僕わからない」と答えます。私はこれを"Search me."と訳しました。

　言うまでもなく、「僕わからない」には数多くの訳し方あります。英語の"search me"は、「わからない」「手がかりがない」という意味のほかに、「私（の中）を探せば、答えが見つかるかもしれない」と、文字通りに受け取ることができるのが魅力の表現です。

　私自身、ミヤザワザワ賢治と呼んでいる人物の作品を読み続けて56年になりますが、本当の幸せは、この「探す」ことにあって、それは今も続いています。私の手から離れるまでのほんの短い間だけ、宮沢賢治がくれたジョバンニの切符をしっかり握りしめているつもりです。

A LESSON IN THE AFTERNOON

"So you see, boys and girls, that is why some have called it a river, while others see a giant trace left by a stream of milk. But does anyone know what really makes up this hazy-white region in the sky?"

The teacher pointed up and down the smoky white zone of the Milky Way that ran across a huge black starmap suspended from the top of the blackboard. He was asking everybody in the class.

Campanella raised his hand, and at that, four or five others also volunteered. Giovanni was about to raise his hand, but suddenly changed his mind.

Giovanni was almost sure that it was all just made up of stars. He had read that in a magazine. But lately Giovanni was sleepy in class nearly every day, had no time to read books and no books to read, and felt, for some reason, that he couldn't properly follow anything anymore.

The teacher noticed this instantly.

"Giovanni, you know what it is, don't you?"

Giovanni stood up courageously. But once on his feet, he wasn't able to give a clear answer. Zanelli, sitting in the seat in front of him, turned around and snickered at him.

Giovanni was flustered, blushing from one ear to the other.

The teacher spoke once again.

"If you were to take a close look at the Milky Way through a big telescope, what would you find it made of?"

Giovanni was now absolutely sure that you'd find stars, but just like the moment before, he couldn't get his answer out.

一、午后の授業

「ではみなさんは、そういうふうに川だと言われたり、乳の流れたあとだと言われたりしていたこのぼんやりと白いものがほんとうは何かご承知ですか。」先生は、黒板に吊した大きな黒い星座の図の、上から下へ白くけぶった銀河帯のようなところを指しながら、みんなに問をかけました。

カムパネルラが手をあげました。それから四五人手をあげました。ジョバンニも手をあげようとして、急いでそのままやめました。たしかにあれがみんな星だと、いつか雑誌で読んだのでしたが、このごろはジョバンニはまるで毎日教室でもねむく、本を読むひまも読む本もないので、なんだかどんなこともよくわからないという気持ちがするのでした。

ところが先生は早くもそれを見附けたのでした。

「ジョバンニさん。あなたはわかっているのでしょう。」

ジョバンニは勢よく立ちあがりましたが、立って見るともうはっきりとそれを答えることができないのでした。ザネリが前の席からふりかえって、ジョバンニを見てくすっとわらいました。ジョバンニはもうどぎまぎしてまっ赤になってしまいました。先生がまた言いました。

「大きな望遠鏡で銀河をよっく調べると銀河は大体何でしょう。」

やっぱり星だとジョバンニは思いましたがこんどもすぐに答えることができませんでした。

*以下、語注の訳の「　」の部分は原作からの引用です。英文と原作の意味がそのまま対応している部分になります。

hazy-white region
「ぼんやりと白いもの」

snickered at... 「〜を見てくすっと笑いました」

flustered 「どぎまぎして」、動揺して

The teacher, perplexed, finally turned his gaze to Campanella. "Well, what about you, Campanella?"

Campanella, who had raised his hand so readily a moment before, just stood in his place fidgeting, unable to answer the question.

The teacher, now more surprised than ever, stared for some time at him.

"All right, then, I'll do it," he hastened to say, pointing to the starmap. "When you look at this hazy-white Milky Way through a good big telescope, the blur is resolved into a great number of tiny stars. Isn't that right, Giovanni?"

Giovanni, now red as a beet, nodded, and before he knew it his eyes were filled with tears and he thought ...

That's right, I knew it all along, and so does Campanella, because it was all in a magazine that we once read together at Campanella's father's house, and he's a scholar!

Campanella leafed through that magazine and then went straight into his father's library, brought a thick book from the shelf, opened it to MILKY WAY, and we spent forever together looking at the lovely photograph of white specks that covered the pitch-black page.

The reason why Campanella didn't answer the teacher right away, even though there was no reason at all for him to forget, is because he feels sorry for me because I have to work hard before and after school and then I feel too down in the dumps to play with everybody or even to talk with him very much.

When Giovanni thought about how Campanella had deliberately not answered out of sympathy for him, he felt indescribably sad both for himself and for Campanella.

The teacher began again.

先生はしばらく困ったようすでしたが、眼をカムパネルラの方へ向けて、

「ではカムパネルラさん。」と名指しました。するとあんなに元気に手をあげたカムパネルラが、やはりもじもじ立ち上ったままやはり答えができませんでした。

先生は意外なようにしばらくじっとカムパネルラを見ていましたが、急いで「では。よし。」と言いながら、自分で星図を指しました。

「このぼんやりと白い銀河を大きないい望遠鏡で見ますと、もうたくさんの小さな星に見えるのです。ジョバンニさんそうでしょう。」

ジョバンニはまっ赤になってうなずきました。けれどもいつかジョバンニの眼のなかには涙がいっぱいになりました。そうだ僕は知っていたのだ、勿論カムパネルラも知っている、それはいつかカムパネルラのお父さんの博士のうちでカムパネルラといっしょに読んだ雑誌のなかにあったのだ。それどこでなくカムパネルラは、その雑誌を読むと、すぐお父さんの書斎から巨きな本をもってきて、ぎんがというところをひろげ、まっ黒な頁いっぱいに白い点々のある美しい写真を二人でいつまでも見たのでした。それをカムパネルラが忘れる筈もなかったのに、すぐに返事をしなかったのは、このごろぼくが、朝にも午后にも仕事がつらく、学校に出てももうみんなともはきはき遊ばず、カムパネルラともあんまり物を言わないようになったので、カムパネルラがそれを知って気の毒がってわざと返事をしなかったのだ、そう考えるとたまらないほど、じぶんもカムパネルラもあわれなような気がするのでした。

先生はまた言いました。

perplexed 「困ったようすで」、当惑して

fidgeting 「もじもじ」、そわそわした様子で

hastened to... 急いで〜した

blur ぼんやりとしているもの

scholar 「博士」、学者

leafed through...
（ページを）パラパラとめくった

white specks 「白い点々」

pitch-black page 「真っ黒な頁」

in the dumps 憂鬱な、落ち込んでいる

deliberately 「わざと」、故意に

"So, if we think of the Milky Way as a Celestial River, then each and every one of these tiny little stars may be seen to be a grain of sand or pebble on the bed of that river. If we imagine it to be a giant stream of milk, then it's even more like a river, and the stars become minute fatty globules floating inside the white liquid.

"Now, ask yourself, what does this liquid actually do, and you will see that it transmits light at a given speed through the void of space, and our Sun and Earth are both floating inside it too. So, you see, we are all living in the liquid of the Celestial River, and when we gaze out from where we are, just as water appears bluest at its deepest spots, so will the places with the most stars look to us the whitest and haziest. That is where the sky's riverbed is the densest and most far reaching. Now look at this model."

The teacher pointed to a large lens that was convex on both sides. Inside the lens were countless grains of sand, all glistening and gleaming.

「ですからもしもこの天の川がほんとうに川だと考える
なら、その一つ一つの小さな星はみんなその川のそこの
砂や砂利の粒にもあたるわけです。またこれを巨きな乳
の流れと考えるならもっと天の川とよく似ています。つ
まりその星はみな、乳のなかにまるで細かにうかんでい
る脂油の球にもあたるのです。そんなら何がその川の水
にあたるかと言いますと、それは真空という光をある速
さで伝えるもので、太陽や地球もやっぱりそのなかに浮
んでいるのです。つまりは私どもも天の川の水のなかに
棲んでいるわけです。そしてその天の川の水のなかから
四方を見ると、ちょうど水が深いほど青く見えるように、
天の川の底の深く遠いところほど星がたくさん集って見
えしたがって白くぼんやり見えるのです。この模型をご
らんなさい。」

　先生は中にたくさん光る砂のつぶの入った大きな両面
の凸レンズを指しました。

Celestial River　「天の
川」

fatty globules　「脂油
の球」

void of space　「真空」、
宇宙空間

haziest　「ぼんやり」

convex　凸状の

glistening　濡れたよう
に光る

gleaming　きらりと光
る

"This closely resembles the shape of the Milky Way. You can think of all these glittering grains of sand as stars, all radiating their own light just as our Sun does. Our Sun lies some distance from the center to the edge, and the Earth is not far away. Now imagine yourself inside this lens at night, looking out. Through this thinner part of the lens you will see only a few grains—stars, I mean—shining.

"But if you look in this direction and in this one, where the glass is thickest, you will see any number of shining grains—stars, I mean—and the farther you look directly into it, the more blurry and milky white everything will appear. That is how we see the Milky Way today. As for the actual size of the lens and the various stars inside it, class time is over now so we'll discuss it all again in our next science lesson.

"And as tonight is the Milky Way Festival, I hope that you will all go outside later and take a good close look at the sky. That's all. Please put away your books and notebooks."

For a while the whole classroom was filled with the sounds of books being stacked and desktops being creaked open and slammed shut. In a moment all stood up as straight as arrows, bowed to the teacher and left.

THE PRINTING HOUSE

As Giovanni was walking out the school gate, seven or eight children from his class were gathering in the yard, forming a circle around Campanella by the cherry blossom tree in the corner. They were no doubt meeting to discuss how to get the big snake gourds they needed to put lights into and float down the river for the star festival that night.

「天の川の形はちょうどこんななのです。このいちいちの光るつぶがみんな私どもの太陽と同じようにじぶんで光っている星だと考えます。私どもの太陽がこのほぼ中ごろにあって地球がそのすぐ近くにあるとします。みなさんは夜にこのまん中に立ってこのレンズの中を見まわすとしてごらんなさい。こっちの方はレンズが薄いのでわずかの光る粒 即ち星しか見えないのでしょう。こっちやこっちの方はガラスが厚いので、光る粒即ち星がたくさん見えその遠いのはぼうっと白く見えるというこれがつまり今日の銀河の説なのです。そんならこのレンズの大きさがどれ位あるかまたその中のさまざまの星についてはもう時間ですからこの次の理科の時間にお話します。では今日はその銀河のお祭なのですからみなさんは外へでてよくそらをごらんなさい。ではここまでです。本やノートをおしまいなさい。」

　そして教室中はしばらく机の蓋をあけたりしめたり本を重ねたりする音がいっぱいでしたがまもなくみんなはきちんと立って礼をすると教室を出ました。

二、活版所

　ジョバンニが学校の門を出るとき、同じ組の七八人は家へ帰らずカムパネルラをまん中にして校庭の隅の桜の木のところに集まっていました。それはこんやの星祭に青いあかりをこしらえて川へ流す烏瓜を取りに行く相談らしかったのです。

blurry 「ぼうっと」

stacked 「重ねた」、積み上げた

creaked open 音を立ててきしみながら開いた

slammed shut バタンと閉めた

THE PRINTING HOUSE 「活版所」

snake gourds 「烏瓜」。ウリ科のつる性多年草。実は楕円形で赤く熟す

銀河鉄道の夜　21

Giovanni hurried out the gate waving his arms. He passed by many houses where people were busily preparing for the Milky Way Festival, hanging decorative bulbs made of yew tree needles from their eaves and fixing lights to the branches of cypress trees.

Without stopping off at home, he turned three corners, entered a large printing house, greeted the man in a baggy white shirt doing accounts by the door, removed his shoes, stepped onto the wooden floor and opened the big door in front of him. Inside all the lights were on even though it was still afternoon, rotary presses were clacking and clanging away, and lots of people with cloth tied around their head or visors perched over their eyes were reading or counting in singsongs and hums.

Giovanni went directly to the man who was sitting at the tall, third desk from the door and bowed to him.

The man rummaged about on one of his shelves for a moment and handed Giovanni a sheet of paper.

"This'd be the amount you might be able to pick," he said.

Giovanni pulled out a small flat box from the foot of the man's desk and went to a spot in a well-lit corner of the room, squatting down beside cases of type propped against the wall. He began to pick tiny type, no larger than grains of millet, with a pair of tweezers.

"Hey, Three-Eyes!" said a man in a blue apron passing behind him. Several men nearby chuckled coldly without saying a word or so much as looking at him.

Giovanni painstakingly picked all his type, rubbing his eyes over and over again.

けれどもジョバンニは手を大きく振ってどしどし学校の門を出て来ました。すると町の家々ではこんやの銀河の祭りにいちいの葉の玉をつるしたりひのきの枝にあかりをつけたりいろいろ仕度をしているのでした。

家へは帰らずジョバンニが町を三つ曲ってある大きな活版処にはいってすぐ入口の計算台に居ただぶだぶの白いシャツを着た人におじぎをしてジョバンニは靴をぬいで上りますと、突き当りの大きな扉をあけました。中にはまだ昼なのに電燈がついてたくさんの輪転器がばたりばたりとまわり、きれで頭をしばったりランプシェードをかけたりした人たちが、何か歌うように読んだり数えたりしながらたくさん働いて居りました。

ジョバンニはすぐ入口から三番目の高い卓子に座った人の所へ行っておじぎをしました。その人はしばらく棚をさがしてから、

「これだけ拾って行けるかね。」と言いながら、一枚の紙切れを渡しました。ジョバンニはその人の卓子の足もとから一つの小さな平たい凾をとりだして向うの電燈のたくさんついた、たてかけてある壁の隅の所へしゃがみ込むと小さなピンセットでまるで栗粒ぐらいの活字を次から次と拾いはじめました。青い胸あてをした人がジョバンニのうしろを通りながら、

「よう、虫めがね君、お早う。」と言いますと、近くの四五人の人たちが声もたてずこっちも向かずに冷くわらいました。

ジョバンニは何べんも眼を拭いながら活字をだんだんひろいました。

yew tree needles 「いちいの葉」

eaves 軒、ひさし

cypress tree 「ひのき」

rotary presses 「輪転機」。円筒形のドラムを回転させながら印刷する機械

clacking and clanging away 「ばたりばたりと」、ガチャガチャと

visors perched over their eyes 「ランプシェードをかけた」。当時イギリスの活版所では、Green-eyeshade と呼ばれるセルロイド製のサンバイザーが使われていた

rummaged about... ～の中をくまなく探した

type 「活字」。活版印刷に用いる凸型の字型

propped against... ～に立てかけた

grains of millet 「栗粒」

tweezers 「ピンセット」

painstakingly 苦労して、入念に、慎重に

Some time after the clock chimed six, having thoroughly compared the flat box full of type with the sheet of paper in his hand, he returned to the man at the tall desk. The man took the box, giving him a slight silent nod. Giovanni bowed, opened the door and went back to the accountant dressed in white who, also without uttering a sound, handed him one little silver coin.

At this Giovanni's face suddenly lit up, he bowed to the accountant in the highest of spirits, took his satchel from the foot of his desk and darted for the door.

From there, whistling cheerfully, he stopped in at the bread shop, bought a small loaf of bread and a bagful of sugar lumps, then sprinted off as fast as his feet would take him.

HOME

The little house that Giovanni came home to in such high spirits was the left one in a row of three located off a back street. Purple kale and asparagus plants were growing in a wooden box beside the door, and shades were rolled down over two little windows.

"I'm back, Mum!" said Giovanni, slipping out of his shoes. "Are you feeling all right?"

"Oh Giovanni, you must have worked so hard today. It has been cool today and I have been feeling just fine."

Giovanni stepped up from the entryway onto the floor. His mother was resting in the front room with a white cloth over her face.

"I bought some sugar lumps today, Mum," he said, opening one of the windows. "I wanted to put a few in your milk for you."

六時がうってしばらくたったころ、ジョバンニは拾った活字をいっぱいに入れた平たい箱をもういちど手にもった紙きれと引き合せてから、さっきの卓子の人へ持って来ました。その人は黙ってそれを受け取って微かにうなずきました。

　ジョバンニはおじぎをすると扉をあけてさっきの計算台のところに来ました。するとさっきの白服を着た人がやっぱりだまって小さな銀貨を一つジョバンニに渡しました。ジョバンニは俄かに顔いろがよくなって威勢よくおじぎをすると台の下に置いた鞄をもっておもてへ飛びだしました。それから元気よく口笛を吹きながらパン屋へ寄ってパンの塊を一つと角砂糖を一袋買いますと一目散に走りだしました。

三、家

　ジョバンニが勢よく帰って来たのは、ある裏町の小さな家でした。その三つならんだ入口の一番左側には空箱に紫いろのケールやアスパラガスが植えてあって小さな二つの窓には日覆いが下りたままになっていました。

　「お母さん。いま帰ったよ。工合悪くなかったの。」ジョバンニは靴をぬぎながら言いました。

　「ああ、ジョバンニ、お仕事がひどかったろう。今日は涼しくてね。わたしはずうっと工合がいいよ。」

　ジョバンニは玄関を上って行きますとジョバンニのお母さんがすぐ入口の室に白い巾を被って寝んでいたのでした。ジョバンニは窓をあけました。

　「お母さん。今日は角砂糖を買ってきたよ。牛乳に入れてあげようと思って。」

sugar lumps 「角砂糖」
satchel 学生かばん

"You eat first, dear. I don't feel like it just now."

"Mum, what time did Sis go back?"

"Oh, around three, I think. She did everything for me."

"Your milk hasn't come, has it?"

"It should have by now," she said.

"I'll go get it for you."

"Don't hurry on my account. You go ahead and eat something first, Giovanni. Your sister cut up some tomatoes and left them there."

"I'll have them then," said Giovanni, taking the plate of tomatoes sitting by the window. "Mum, I'm sure dad will be coming home soon now," he added, munching hungrily on the tomatoes and a piece of bread.

"Yes, I think so too. But why are you so sure?"

"Because it said in this morning's paper that the catch up in the north was really great."

"But, you know, your father may not have gone fishing up there."

"No, he's out there all right. Dad couldn't have done anything bad enough that they had to send him to prison or something for. It wasn't all that long ago that he came to our school and donated all those things like that huge crab shell and those reindeer horns. They're still keeping them in the specimen room. All the sixth-grade pupils get to see them when the teacher brings them one at a time to the classroom. Year before last, on a school excursion ..."

"Your father promised to bring you back an otter coat the next time he came back, didn't he?"

「ああ、お前さきにおあがり。あたしはまだほしくないんだから。」

「お母さん。姉さんはいつ帰ったの。」

「ああ三時ころ帰ったよ。みんなそこらをしてくれてね。」

「お母さんの牛乳は来ていないんだろうか。」

「来なかったろうかねえ。」

「ぼく行ってとって来よう。」

「ああたしはゆっくりでいいんだからお前さきにおあがり、姉さんがね、トマトで何かこしらえてそこへ置いて行ったよ。」

「ではぼくたべよう。」

ジョバンニは窓のところからトマトの皿をとってパンといっしょにしばらくむしゃむしゃたべました。

「ねえお母さん。ぼくお父さんはきっと間もなく帰ってくると思うよ。」

「ああたしもそう思う。けれどもおまえはどうしてそう思うの。」

「だって今朝の新聞に今年は北の方の漁は大へんよかったと書いてあったよ。」

「ああだけどねえ、お父さんは漁へ出ていないかもしれない。」

「きっと出ているよ。お父さんが監獄へ入るようなそんな悪いことをした筈がないんだ。この前お父さんが持ってきて学校へ寄贈した巨きな蟹の甲らだのとなかいの角だの今だってみんな標本室にあるんだ。六年生なんか授業のとき先生がかわるがわる教室へ持って行くよ。一昨年修学旅行で〔以下数文字分空白〕

「お父さんはこの次はおまえにラッコの上着をもってくるといったねえ。」

on my account　私のために

catch　「漁」

specimen room　「標本室」

otter coat　「ラッコの上着」

"All the kids make fun of me about that every time they see me."

"Do they say nasty things to you?"

"Yeah, except for Campanella. He never says nasty things. Whenever somebody does, he always looks really sorry for me."

"Your father and Campanella's father were close friends just like you two when they were little."

"Oh, that's why dad used to take me sometimes to Campanella's house. Everything was so good then. I used to go lots of times on my way home from school. They had a train that ran on an alcohol burner. When you hooked up seven rails it made a circle with telegraph poles and signals, and the train could only go when the signal light turned green. Once we ran out of alcohol so we put in some kerosene, but the little boiler got all sooty."

"Did it now..."

"It's always so quiet there when I pass by every morning delivering the paper."

"That's because it's still early."

"They've got a dog named Sauer and he's got a tail just like a broom. He yelps and sniffs and when I'm there he follows me all the way to the end of the street. Sometimes he even follows me further. Tonight everybody's going to make lanterns out of snake gourds and float them down the river. I'll bet anything that dog will follow us."

"That's right, tonight was the Milky Way Festival."

"Uh-huh. I'll go get your milk and have a look on the way back."

"All right, you do that. But don't go on the river, Giovanni."

「みんながぼくにあうとそれを言うよ。ひやかすように言うんだ。」

「おまえに悪口を言うの。」

「うん、けれどもカムパネルラなんか決して言わない。カムパネルラはみんながそんなことを言うときは気の毒そうにしているよ。」

「あの人はうちのお父さんとはちょうどおまえたちのように小さいときからのお友達だったそうだよ。」

「ああだからお父さんはぼくをつれてカムパネルラのうちへもつれて行ったよ。あのころはよかったなあ。ぼくは学校から帰る途中たびたびカムパネルラのうちに寄った。カムパネルラのうちにはアルコールランプで走る汽車があったんだ。レールを七つ組み合せると円くなってそれに電柱や信号標もついていて信号標のあかりは汽車が通るときだけ青くなるようになっていたんだ。いつかアルコールがなくなったとき石油をつかったら、罐がすっかり煤けたよ。」

「そうかねえ。」

「いまも毎朝新聞をまわしに行くよ。けれどもいつでも家中まだしぃんとしているからな。」

「早いからねえ。」

「ザウエルという犬がいるよ。しっぽがまるで箒のようだ。ぼくが行くと鼻を鳴らしてついてくるよ。ずうっと町の角までついてくる。もっとついてくることもあるよ。今夜はみんなで烏瓜のあかりを川へながしに行くんだって。きっと犬もついて行くよ。」

「そうだ。今晩は銀河のお祭だねえ。」

「うん。ぼく牛乳をとりながら見てくるよ。」

「ああ行っておいで。川へははいらないでね。」

telegraph poles 「電柱」

kerosene 「石油」、灯油

sooty 「煤けた」

"I'll just watch from the bank. I'll only be gone an hour."

"You don't have to come back so soon. I'm not worried so long as you're with Campanella."

"Oh, we'll be together all right. Should I close the window for you, Mum?"

"Well, let me see ... it's already getting cool now, I suppose."

Giovanni rose, closed the window, and put away his plate and the remaining bread.

"Then I'll be back in an hour and a half," he said, whipping his shoes on.

He passed through the dark doorway.

NIGHT OF THE CENTAUR FESTIVAL

With his lips puckered as if he was whistling some sad song, Giovanni came walking toward town, down a slope that was a pitch-black tunnel of thickly growing cypresses.

A single tall street lamp, radiating a brilliant yet soft light, stood at the foot of the slope. As he made his way steadily toward the lamp, his shadow, which had been trailing behind him like a lanky blurry murky ghost, became darker and more distinct, kicking up its legs and swinging its arms until turning around to his side.

I'm a great locomotive! I'm speeding up here because this is an incline. I'm going to pass that lamppost any second now. Hey, now my shadow's the needle of a compass. It's gone around in a circle and now it's right in front of me!

「ああぼく岸から見るだけなんだ。一時間で行ってくるよ。」

「もっと遊んでおいで。カムパネルラさんと一緒なら心配はないから。」

「ああきっと一緒だよ。お母さん、窓をしめて置こうか。」

「ああ、どうか。もう涼しいからね」

ジョバンニは立って窓をしめお皿やパンの袋を片附けると勢よく靴をはいて

「では一時間半で帰ってくるよ。」と言いながら暗い戸口を出ました。

四、ケンタウル祭の夜

ジョバンニは、口笛を吹いているようなさびしい口付きで、檜のまっ黒にならんだ町の坂を下りて来たのでした。

坂の下に大きな一つの街燈が、青白く立派に光って立っていました。ジョバンニが、どんどん電燈の方へ下りて行きますと、いままでばけもののように、長くぼんやり、うしろへ引いていたジョバンニの影ぼうしは、だんだん濃く黒くはっきりなって、足をあげたり手を振ったり、ジョバンニの横の方へまわって来るのでした。

（ぼくは立派な機関車だ。ここは勾配だから速いぞ。ぼくはいまその電燈を通り越す。そうら、こんどはぼくの影法師はコムパスだ。あんなにくるっとまわって、前の方へ来た。）

bank 「岸」

whipping さっと動く、急に動く

CENTAUR FESTIVAL 「ケンタウル祭」。南半球の星座のケンタウルス座を祭りの名に用いたといわれる

puckered （唇などを）すぼめた

pitch-black 真っ黒な。この場合の pitch は石油タールなどを蒸留した後に残る黒色のカスで道路の舗装にも用いるものを指している

lanky ひょろ長い

murky 暗い、見通せない

That is what Giovanni was thinking as he took giant steps beneath the street lamp. Just then Zanelli, who had sniggered at him in class that day, came out of a dark alleyway on the other side of the post. He was wearing a new shirt with pointed collars, and he all but collided with Giovanni as their paths crossed.

Giovanni was about to say, "Zanelli, are you going to the river to float gourds?" But before he could get the words out, Zanelli hollered nastily from behind, "Giovanni's getting an otter coat from his father!"

Giovanni's heart suddenly went cold and he heard a ringing in his ears coming from all around him.

"Who do you think you are, Zanelli!" he screamed back. But Zanelli had already disappeared into a house with a cypress tree in front.

Why does he keep saying those things when I haven't done anything to him? He looks just like a rat when he runs away like that. He's so stupid, that's his problem!

Giovanni's mind was leaping from one thing to another as he passed through town with all the houses decorated in the most beautiful array of ornamented branches and lights.

The watchmaker's shop had a radiant fluorescent light in the window and an owl, made of stone, whose red eyes rolled around every second. All kinds of jewels were piled on a platter made of thick glass the color of the sea. The platter rotated, revolving the starlike jewels and bringing a copper centaur around from the other side. Between the centaur and the jewels there was a circular black map of the heavens decorated with blue asparagus leaves.

Giovanni forgot himself in the map of the heavens.

とジョバンニが思いながら、大股にその街燈の下を通り過ぎたとき、いきなりひるまのザネリが、新らしいえりの尖ったシャツを着て電燈の向う側の暗い小路から出て来て、ひらっとジョバンニとすれちがいました。

「ザネリ、烏瓜ながしに行くの。」ジョバンニがまだそう言ってしまわないうちに、

「ジョバンニ、お父さんから、らっこの上着が来るよ。」その子が投げつけるようにうしろから叫びました。

ジョバンニは、ばっと胸がつめたくなり、そこら中きぃんと鳴るように思いました。

「何だい。ザネリ。」とジョバンニは高く叫び返しましたがもうザネリは向うのひばの植った家の中へはいっていました。

「ザネリはどうしてぼくがなんにもしないのにあんなことを言うのだろう。走るときはまるで鼠のようなくせに。ぼくがなんにもしないのにあんなことを言うのはザネリがばかなからだ。」

ジョバンニは、せわしくいろいろのことを考えながら、さまざまの灯や木の枝で、すっかりきれいに飾られた街を通って行きました。時計屋の店には明るくネオン燈がついて、一秒ごとに石でこさえたふくろうの赤い眼が、くるっくるっとうごいたり、いろいろな宝石が海のような色をした厚い硝子の盤に載って星のようにゆっくり循ったり、また向う側から、銅の人馬がゆっくりこっちへまわって来たりするのでした。そのまん中に円い黒い星座早見が青いアスパラガスの葉で飾ってありました。

ジョバンニはわれを忘れて、その星座の図に見入りました。

all but...　〜も同然で

collided with...　〜とぶつかった

sniggered at...　〜を見てくすくす笑った

hollered　叫んだ、どなった

leaping from one thing to another　次から次へと飛躍する

fluorescent　蛍光の

platter　「盤」

copper centaur　「銅の人馬」、銅のケンタウルス

circular black map of the heavens　「円い黒い星座早見表」

銀河鉄道の夜　33

It was much much smaller than the star chart that he had seen at school earlier that day. But with this one all you had to do was to set the date and time by turning the platter, and the sky for that night would appear in the oval opening. The Milky Way ran straight through the middle, a smoky zone of white stretching from one end to the other with what looked like steamy vapors rising, as if after an explosion, from the bottom reaches.

In the depths of the shop stood a small telescope on a glowing yellow tripod and behind that, on the back wall, hung a big map depicting the entire sky in constellations of bizarre beasts, snakes, fish and bottle shapes. Giovanni wondered if the sky was really so crammed with scorpions and brave warriors and things, and he thought, standing there in a daze ...

Ah, I'd like nothing more than to travel inside there as far as a human could go!

Then suddenly he remembered the milk for his mother and he walked away from the watchmaker's shop. He went through town swinging his arms and deliberately straining to swell up his chest, even though the shoulders of his coat were pinching him.

それはひる学校で見たあの図よりはずうっと小さかったのですがその日と時間に合せて盤をまわすと、そのとき出ているそらがそのまま楕円形《だえんけい》のなかにめぐってあらわれるようになって居《お》りやはりそのまん中には上から下へかけて銀河がぼうとけむったような帯になってその下の方ではかすかに爆発して湯気でもあげているように見えるのでした。またそのうしろには三本の脚のついた小さな望遠鏡が黄いろに光って立っていましたしいちばんうしろの壁には空じゅうの星座をふしぎな獣《けもの》や蛇《へび》や魚や瓶《びん》の形に書いた大きな図がかかっていました。ほんとうにこんなような蝎《さそり》だの勇士だのそらにぎっしり居るだろうか、ああぼくはその中をどこまでも歩いて見たいと思ってたりしてしばらくぼんやり立って居ました。

　それから俄《にわ》かにお母さんの牛乳のことを思いだしてジョバンニはその店をはなれました。そしてきゅうくつな上着の肩を気にしながらそれでもわざと胸を張って大きく手を振って町を通って行きました。

tripod　三脚

depicting　〜を描いた
constellations　「星座」

bizarre　「不思議な」、奇怪な、異様な

crammed with...　〜でぎっしりの、〜詰まった

in a daze　「ぼんやり」

deliberately　「わざと」

straining to...　〜までピンと張る、張り切って〜する

swell up his chest
胸を大きく脹らませる

pinching　締め付けて

The air was crystal clear, flowing through the streets and past the shops as if it was water. Street lamps were tucked away among the blue branches of fir and oak, and the six plane trees in front of the Electric Company, decked inside, outside and everywhere with miniature light bulbs, made the whole place look like Mermaid City under the sea.

All of the children, dressed in freshly pressed kimonos, were running about, shouting and whistling the tune of "Once Around the Stars."

"O Centaurus, Let the Dew Fall!"

As they played happily, fireworks of blue magnesium burned in the sky.

But Giovanni, his head drooping down, was lost in thoughts far away from that lively atmosphere about him. He hurried in the direction of the dairy.

He found himself on the edge of town where countless poplar trees stood as if floating up into the starry sky. He opened the darkened gate of the dairy and waited by the dusky kitchen, which smelled of cows.

"Good evening," he called out, removing his cap.

It looked quiet inside, and there wasn't a soul in sight.

"Good evening," he called loudly again, standing up very straight. "Anybody home?"

After a while an old woman shuffled out. She did not look well at all, and mumbled to herself, "What d'ya want?"

"Um, we didn't get any milk at my place today," said Giovanni in a spirited voice, "so I'm here to fetch it."

fir 「もみ」

oak 「楢」

tucked away 隠れて

decked 飾られた

Mermaid City under the sea 「人魚の都」

"Once Around the Stars" 「星めぐりの歌」（宮沢賢治作詞・作曲の歌）

drooping down 「垂れて」

dairy 「牛乳屋」

dusky 薄暗い

there wasn't a soul in sight （見渡す限り）人っ子一人いなかった

shuffled out 足を引きずりながら出てきた

fetch 取ってくる

a patch of skin 皮膚の一部分（patch: 他の部分とは様子が異なる部分）

　空気は澄みきって、まるで水のように通りや店の中を流れましたし、街燈はみなまっ青なもみや楢の枝で包まれ、電気会社の前の六本のプラタヌスの木などは、中に沢山の豆電燈がついて、ほんとうにそこらは人魚の都のように見えるのでした。子どもらは、みんな新らしい折のついた着物を着て、星めぐりの口笛を吹いたり、

　「ケンタウルス、露をふらせ。」と叫んで走ったり、青いマグネシヤの花火を燃したりして、たのしそうに遊んでいるのでした。けれどもジョバンニは、いつかまた深く首を垂れて、そこらのにぎやかさとはまるでちがったことを考えながら、牛乳屋の方へ急ぐのでした。

　ジョバンニは、いつか町はずれのポプラの木が幾本も幾本も、高く星ぞらに浮んでいるところに来ていました。その牛乳屋の黒い門を入り、牛の匂のするうすくらい台所の前に立って、ジョバンニは帽子をぬいで「今晩は、」と言いましたら、家の中はしぃんとして誰も居たようではありませんでした。

　「今晩は、ごめんなさい。」ジョバンニはまっすぐに立ってまた叫びました。するとしばらくたってから、年老った女の人が、どこか工合が悪いようにそろそろと出て来て何か用かと口の中で言いました。

　「あの、今日、牛乳が僕んとこへ来なかったので、貰いにあがったんです。」ジョバンニが一生けん命勢よく言いました。

The old woman scratched a patch of skin under her red eye and looked down at Giovanni.

"No one around here now, and I dunno. Come back tomorrow," she said.

"But my mum's sick, so we must have it by tonight."

"Well, in that case come back a little later."

The old woman was almost gone when Giovanni called out, "A little later? ... well, thank you!" He bowed and left.

When Giovanni was about to turn the corner into town he noticed six or seven boys in front of the grocer's on the road to the bridge. Their black shapes mingled with their dimly glowing white shirts. They were each carrying a lighted gourd lantern, whistling and laughing.

There was no mistaking those whistles and laughs. They belonged to Giovanni's classmates. At first Giovanni, startled, started to turn back, but then he changed his mind and headed for the bridge with very sure strides.

"Going to the river?" That's what he wanted to say, but the words got stuck in his throat, and before he could say anything at all, Zanelli hollered.

"Giovanni's getting an otter coat!"

Everyone immediately joined in.

"Giovanni's getting an otter coat!"

Giovanni, blushing to his ears, started to walk. He was already past them when he noticed Campanella standing tall among them. Campanella was keeping silent, with a smile of soft compassion on his lips, no doubt worried that Giovanni might take offense at the others' words.

「いま誰もいないでわかりません。あしたにして下さい。」

その人は、赤い眼の下のとこを擦りながら、ジョバンニを見おろして言いました。

「おっかさんが病気なんですから今晩でないと困るんです。」

「ではもう少したってから来てください。」その人はもう行ってしまいそうでした。

「そうですか。ではありがとう。」ジョバンニは、お辞儀をして台所から出ました。

十字になった町のかどを、まがろうとしましたら、向うの橋へ行く方の雑貨店の前で、黒い影やぼんやり白いシャツが入り乱れて、六七人の生徒らが、口笛を吹いたり笑ったりして、めいめい烏瓜の燈火を持ってやって来るのを見ました。その笑い声も口笛も、みんな聞きおぼえのあるものでした。ジョバンニの同級の子供らだったのです。ジョバンニは思わずどきっとして戻ろうとしましたが、思い直して、一そう勢よくそっちへ歩いて行きました。

「川へ行くの。」ジョバンニが言おうとして、少しのどがつまったように思ったとき、

「ジョバンニ、らっこの上着が来るよ。」さっきのザネリがまた叫びました。

「ジョバンニ、らっこの上着が来るよ。」すぐみんなが、続いて叫びました。ジョバンニはまっ赤になって、もう歩いているかもわからず、急いで行きすぎようとしましたら、そのなかにカムパネルラが居たのです。カムパネルラは気の毒そうに、だまって少しわらって、怒らないだろうかというようにジョバンニの方を見ていました。

mingled 「入り乱れて」、混ざった

with very sure strides 「勢よく」、しっかりした足取りで

take offense at... （嫌な言動など）に怒る

Giovanni avoided Campanella's gaze, and as he left his friend behind he heard the others break out in their loud whistling again. He turned the corner, looking back at them and saw Zanelli looking back too. Campanella, now whistling with all his might, was disappearing into the milky-white haze surrounding the bridge.

Giovanni, overwhelmed by sadness, began to run out of the blue, as all the little children, who thought Giovanni funny as he ran, hopped about on one leg, screaming, yelling and hooting with their hands over their ears.

In an instant he found himself hurrying toward a black hill.

THE WEATHER STATION PILLAR

Beyond the pasture the hills rolled on one after another, while their flat blackened peaks seemed to be lined up lower than usual, dim and hazy below the Big Dipper in the northern sky.

Giovanni was already deep inside a grove of trees that were dripping with dew. He climbed steadily up a straight and narrow path illuminated by starlight, the single clearing in a thicket of dark plants taking on all shapes and sizes. There were tiny insects gleaming blue amid the bushes, rendering their leaves transparent blue and reminding him of the snake gourd lanterns all the children had been carrying.

ジョバンニは、遁げるようにその眼を避け、そしてカムパネルラのせいの高いかたちが過ぎて行って間もなく、みんなはてんでに口笛を吹きました。町かどを曲るとき、ふりかえって見ましたら、ザネリがやはりふりかえって見ていました。そしてカムパネルラもまた、高く口笛を吹いて向うにぼんやり見える橋の方へ歩いて行ってしまったのでした。ジョバンニは、なんとも言えずさびしくなって、いきなり走り出しました。すると耳に手をあてて、わあっと言いながら片足でぴょんぴょん跳んでいた小さな子供らは、ジョバンニが面白くてかけるのだと思ってわあいと叫びました。まもなくジョバンニは黒い丘の方へ急ぎました。

五、天気輪の柱

牧場のうしろはゆるい丘になって、その黒い平らな頂上は、北の大熊星の下に、ぼんやりふだんよりも低く連って見えました。

ジョバンニは、もう露の降りかかった小さな林のこみちを、どんどんのぼって行きました。まっくらな草や、いろいろな形に見えるやぶのしげみの間を、その小さなみちが、一すじ白く星あかりに照らしだされてあったのです。草の中には、ぴかぴか青びかりを出す小さな虫もいて、ある葉は青くすかし出され、ジョバンニは、さっきみんなの持って行った烏瓜のあかりのようだとも思いました。

with all his might　力いっぱい、精一杯

out of the blue　「いきなり」、突然

hooting　やじる、わめく

WEATHER STATION PILLAR　「天気輪の柱」。「天気輪」については、さまざまな説がある。「天気柱」であれば、東北地方で農耕に恵みをもたらすよう天候を祈り、死者を弔う目的で設置された仏教由来の建造物。英訳に station が入っているのは、各駅停車する駅のイメージ

Big Dipper　北斗七星

grove　「林」、木立

dew　「露」

thicket　「しげみ」、雑木林

rendering　〜の状態にする

transparent　透き通った

Giovanni came out of the pitch-black pine and oak wood, and all of a sudden there was a vast sky above him, with the Milky Way, soft and blurry white, streaming from south to north.

He could make out the pillar of the weather station at the top of a slope that was a carpet of daisies and bellflowers. Their fragrance was so strong that he felt you could smell it through a dream. A single bird passed over him, crying above the hill.

Giovanni came to the base of the weather station pillar at the very top of the hill and, shuddering, plopped down into the cold grass. The lights of the town below were burning through the darkness as if the town itself was a miniature shrine at the bottom of the sea. He could faintly catch snatches of children's screams and bits of whistles and songs. The wind howled far away and all the hill's plant life rustled. His sweat-soaked shirt started to give him a chill as he looked down on the distant swept-black field from the edge of town.

The sound of a train came to him from the field. It was a little train with a single row of tiny red windows, and inside it all of the passengers were peeling apples, laughing or doing one thing and another. This made Giovanni feel immensely sad, and he once again gazed up at the sky.

But no matter how hard he looked at the sky, he just couldn't see the cold barren place that the teacher had described in class. On the contrary, the more deeply he stared into it, the more he saw a field with little groves of trees and pastures. Then he noticed the blue stars of Lyra, the Harp, multiplying, twinkling all the while, and the Harp itself stretching out its legs then pulling them in until it looked like a long mushroom.

And from where he was down to the town below, everything appeared to be a blurry cluster of countless stars … or a single vast puff of smoke.

そのまっ黒な、松や楢の林を越えると、俄かにがらんと空がひらけて、天の川がしらしらと南から北へ亘っているのが見え、また頂の、天気輪の柱も見わけられたのでした。つりがねそうか野ぎくかの花が、そこらいちめんに、夢の中からでも薫りだしたというように咲き、鳥が一疋、丘の上を鳴き続けながら通って行きました。

ジョバンニは、頂の天気輪の柱の下に来て、どかどかするからだを、つめたい草に投げました。

町の灯は、暗の中をまるで海の底のお宮のけしきのようにともり、子供らの歌う声や口笛、きれぎれの叫び声もかすかに聞えて来るのでした。風が遠くで鳴り、丘の草もしずかにそよぎ、ジョバンニの汗でぬれたシャツもつめたく冷されました。ジョバンニは町のはずれから遠く黒くひろがった野原を見わたしました。

そこから汽車の音が聞えてきました。その小さな列車の窓は一列小さく赤く見え、その中にはたくさんの旅人が、苹果を剥いたり、わらったり、いろいろな風にしていると考えますと、ジョバンニは、もう何とも言えずかなしくなって、また眼をそらに挙げました。

ああああの白いそらの帯がみんな星だというぞ。

ところがいくら見ていても、そのそらはひる先生の言ったような、がらんとした冷いとこだとは思われませんでした。それどころでなく、見れば見るほど、そこは小さな林や牧場やらある野原のように考えられて仕方なかったのです。そしてジョバンニは青い琴の星が、三つにも四つにもなって、ちらちら瞬き、脚が何べんも出たり引っ込んだりして、とうとう茸のように長く延びるのを見ました。またすぐ眼の下のまちまでがやっぱりぼんやりしたたくさんの星の集りか一つの大きなけむりかのように見えるように思いました。

bellflowers 「つりがねそう」、カンパニュラ

plopped down どしんと座った、体を投げ出した

miniature shrine 「お宮」、小さな神社、祭壇

snatches 断片、「きれぎれの叫び声」

rustled そよいだ、サラサラと鳴った

immensely とてつもなく、非常に

cold barren place 「がらんとした冷たいとこ」（barren: 不毛の）

Lyra 琴座

MILKY WAY STATION

Then Giovanni saw the weather station pillar right behind him take on the vague shape of a triangular turret, flickering on and off like a firefly. When the blur in his eyes passed, everything became clear and finely outlined, and the turret with its light soared straight up into the dense cobalt-blue field of the sky that was like a sheet of freshly tempered steel. Out of the blue he was sure he heard a strange voice calling ...

"Milky Way Station! Milky Way Station!"

And before his eyes there was a flash flood of intensely bright light, as if billions and billions of phosphorescent cuttlefish had fossilized at their most radiant instant and been plunged into the sky, or as if someone had discovered a hidden cache of precious jewels that the Diamond Company had been hoarding to bolt the price sky high, turning the whole treasure topsy-turvy and lavishing them throughout the heavens. Giovanni found himself rubbing his eyes over and over, blinded by the sudden dazzle.

By the time he came to, he had, for some time now, been chugging along on the little train. It was really him on the nighttime narrow-gauge railroad, gazing out the window of a wagon with its little row of yellow lights. Inside, the seats, nearly all empty, were covered in blue velvet, and two big brass buttons gleamed on the varnished gray wall opposite him.

六、銀河ステーション

　そしてジョバンニはすぐうしろの天気輪の柱がいつか
ぼんやりした三角標の形になって、しばらく蛍のように、
ぺかぺか消えたりともったりしているのを見ました。そ
れはだんだんはっきりして、とうとうりんとうごかない
ようになり、濃い鋼青のそらの野原にたちました。いま
新らしく灼いたばかりの青い鋼の板のような、そらの野
原に、まっすぐにすきっと立ったのです。

　するとどこかで、ふしぎな声が、銀河ステーション、
銀河ステーションと言う声がしたと思うといきなり眼の
前が、ぱっと明るくなって、まるで億万の蛍烏賊の火を
一ぺんに化石させて、そら中に沈めたという工合、また
ダイアモンド会社で、ねだんがやすくならないために、
わざと穫れないふりをして、かくして置いた金剛石を、
誰かがいきなりひっくりかえして、ばら撒いたという風
に、眼の前がさあっと明るくなって、ジョバンニは、思
わず何べんも眼を擦ってしまいました。

　気がついてみると、さっきから、ごとごとごとごと、ジョ
バンニの乗っている小さな列車が走りつづけていたので
した。ほんとうにジョバンニは、夜の軽便鉄道の、小さ
な黄いろの電燈のならんだ車室に、窓から外を見ながら
座っていたのです。車室の中は、青い天蚕絨を張った腰
掛けが、まるでがら明きで、向うの鼠いろのワニスを塗っ
た壁に　は、真鍮の大きなぼたんが二つ光っているので
した。

<triangular turret 「三角標」、三角覘標（turret: 小塔）

freshly tempered 「灼いたばかりの」

phosphorescent 燐光を発する、青光りする

cuttlefish 「烏賊」

fossilized 化石化する

plunged into... 「沈めた」、～に飛び込んだ、～に突入した

cache 隠し場所

hoarding ため込む、貯蔵する

topsy-turvy 「ひっくりかえして」、逆さまの

lavishing 気前よく与える

dazzle まぶしい光

chugging ガタゴト走る

brass 「真鍮」

varnished ニスを塗った

銀河鉄道の夜　45

Giovanni noticed a tall boy in a glistening jet-black jacket poking his head out the window in the seat directly in front of him. He could have sworn, judging from the boy's shoulders, that he had seen him somewhere before. He wanted to know who it was so much that he couldn't stand it. But just as he was about to stick his own head out his window and take a look, the boy popped his in and turned toward him.

It was Campanella!

Giovanni was about to ask him if he had been on the train from the very beginning, but Campanella spoke up sooner.

"Everybody ran so fast but they missed the train. Even Zanelli ran like mad but he couldn't catch up with me."

Giovanni thought to himself ... I got it! We've been asked to go away together.

But he said, "Should we wait for them somewhere down the line?"

"Zanelli went home already," said Campanella. "His father came to get him."

Campanella's face turned pale, as if something was hurting him. Giovanni felt funny inside, as though he couldn't remember something that he had somewhere forgotten.

すぐ前の席に、ぬれたようにまっ黒な上着を着た、せいの高い子供が、窓から頭を出して外を見ているのに気が付きました。そしてそのこどもの肩のあたりが、どうも見たことのあるような気がして、そう思うと、もうどうしても誰だかわかりたくて、たまらなくなりました。いきなりこっちも窓から顔を出そうとしたとき、俄かにその子供が頭を引っ込めて、こっちを見ました。

　それはカムパネルラだったのです。

　ジョバンニが、カムパネルラ、きみは前からここに居たのと言おうと思ったとき、カムパネルラが

　「みんなはねずいぶん走ったけれども遅れてしまったよ。ザネリもね、ずいぶん走ったけれども追いつかなかった。」と言いました。

　ジョバンニは、（そうだ、ぼくたちはいま、いっしょにさそって出掛けたのだ。）とおもいながら、

　「どこかで待っていようか。」と言いました。するとカムパネルラは

　「ザネリはもう帰ったよ。お父さんが迎いにきたんだ。」

　カムパネルラは、なぜかそう言いながら、少し顔いろが青ざめて、どこか苦しいというふうでした。するとジョバンニも、なんだかどこかに、何か忘れたものがあるというような、おかしな気持ちがしてだまってしまいました。

jet-black 「真っ黒な」、漆黒の

felt funny 「おかしな気持ちがして」、変な感じがした、様子が変だった、気分が悪買った

銀河鉄道の夜　47

"Oh, gee," said Campanella, coming alive and peering out the window again. "I've forgotten my water bottle. And I've forgotten my sketchbook too. Well, no matter, we'll be coming into Swan Station soon. There's nothing I like better than watching swans. I'm sure I'll be able to see them no matter how far down the river they fly."

Campanella looked down at the round plate-like map in his hand, busily turning it round and round. On the map a single track of rail skirted the left bank of the whitened Milky Way, tracing its way south and further south again. But the really fantastic thing was that the map, a platter black as night itself, was inlaid with little whistle stops and triangular turrets one after the other, and forests and miniature lakes, all shining beautifully in blue, green and bitter orange.

Giovanni was sure he had seen that map somewhere before.

"Where did you buy that map?" he asked. "It's made of obsidian, isn't it?"

"I got it at Milky Way Station. You mean, you didn't get one too?"

"Gee, I'm not sure if I went through Milky Way Station. We're around here now, aren't we?" said Giovanni, pointing to a place directly north of a sign that read SWAN STATION.

"That's right," said Campanella. "Oh, good heavens! I wonder if that dry river bed is just moonlight."

When the two of them looked they saw the pale bank of the Milky Way glittering with pampas grass growing all along it, rustling and swishing, rolling in the wind into billows of waves in a silver sky.

ところがカムパネルラは、窓から外をのぞきながら、もうすっかり元気が直って、勢よく言いました。

「ああしまった。ぼく、水筒を忘れてきた。スケッチ帳も忘れてきた。けれど構わない。もうじき白鳥の停車場だから。ぼく、白鳥を見るなら、ほんとうにすきだ。川の遠くを飛んでいたって、ぼくはきっと見える。」そして、カムパネルラは、円い板のようになった地図を、しきりにぐるぐるまわして見ていました。まったくその中に、白くあらわされた天の川の左の岸に沿って一条の鉄道線路が、南へ南へとたどって行くのでした。そしてその地図の立派なことは、夜のようにまっ黒な盤の上に、一一の停車場や三角標、泉水や森が、青や橙や緑や、うつくしい光でちりばめられてありました。ジョバンニはなんだかその地図をどこかで見たようにおもいました。

「この地図はどこで買ったの。黒曜石でできてるねえ。」

ジョバンニが言いました。

「銀河ステーションで、もらったんだ。君もらわなかったの。」

「ああ、ぼく銀河ステーションを通ったろうか。いまぼくたちの居るとこ、ここだろう。」

ジョバンニは、白鳥と書いてある停車場のしるしの、すぐ北を指しました。

「そうだ。おや、あの河原は月夜だろうか。」

そっちを見ますと、青白く光る銀河の岸に、銀いろの空のすすきが、もうまるでいちめん、風にさらさらさらさら、ゆられてうごいて、波を立てているのでした。

Swan Station 「白鳥の停車場」

skirted 「に沿って」

whistle stops 小駅

obsidian 「黒曜石」。火山岩の一種。外見は黒色で、鋭いガラス質であることから刃物などに使われた

pampas grass 「すすき」

swishing （風などが）ヒュっと鳴る

billows of waves 大きくうねる波

"That's not moonlight," said Giovanni. "It's shining because it's the Milky Way!"

Giovanni felt so elated, he wanted to jump up and down. He tapped his feet, poked his head out the window and, standing as tall as he could on tiptoes, whistled the tune of "Once Around the Stars."

He couldn't get a clear picture of the water in the river no matter how hard he looked at it. He kept staring and staring until he gradually saw that the clear water was even more crystal than glass, even more transparent than hydrogen. Maybe it was just his eyes, but the water in spots seemed to be making delicate purple ripples or glimmering rainbows of light as it flowed steadily, silently along. Phosphorescent triangular turrets, perfectly erect, patched the sky.

The faraway turrets were small, the closer ones large; the faraway ones distinctly yellow and bitter orange, the closer ones pale and faintly hazy. Some turrets were triangular, others rectangular; some the shape of chains, others the shape of lightning. But they were all in lines, flooding the field with light.

Giovanni felt more excited than he had ever been, and he shook his head for all he was worth. Then, as far and as wide as his eyes could see, the blues and oranges and all the luminescent turrets began to sway and flicker, as if they were alive and breathing themselves.

"I've made it right into the sky's field!" cried Giovanni. He leaned out the window and pointed to the front of the train with his left hand, adding, "Oh, this train isn't burning coal!"

"Must run on alcohol or electricity," said Campanella.

The beautiful little train, chugging and clanking its way along the pampas grass that waved in the sky, through the waters of the Milky Way and the glimmering milky-white light of triangulation pillars, was running on its endless journey.

「月夜でないよ。銀河だから光るんだよ。」ジョバンニは言いながら、まるではね上りたいくらい愉快になって、足をこつこつ鳴らし、窓から顔を出して、高く高く星めぐりの口笛を吹きながら一生けん命延びあがって、その天の川の水を、見きわめようとしましたが、はじめはどうしてもそれが、はっきりしませんでした。けれどもだんだん気をつけて見ると、そのきれいな水は、ガラスよりも水素よりもすきとおって、ときどき眼の加減か、ちらちら紫いろのこまかな波をたてたり、虹のようにぎらっと光ったりしながら、声もなくどんどん流れて行き、野原にはあっちにもこっちにも、燐光の三角標が、うつくしく立っていたのです。遠いものは小さく、近いものは大きく、遠いものは橙や黄いろではっきりし、近いものは青白く少しかすんで、或いは三角形、或いは四辺形、あるいは電や鎖の形、さまざまにならんで、野原いっぱい光っているのでした。ジョバンニは、まるでどきどきして、頭をやけに振りました。するとほんとうに、そのきれいな野原中の青や橙や、いろいろかがやく三角標も、てんでに息をつくように、ちらちらゆれたり顫えたりしました。

「ぼくはもう、すっかり天の野原に来た。」ジョバンニは言いました。

「それにこの汽車石炭をたいていないねえ。」ジョバンニが左手をつき出して窓から前の方を見ながら言いました。

「アルコールか電気だろう。」カムパネルラが言いました。

ごとごとごとごと、その小さなきれいな汽車は、そらのすすきの風にひるがえる中を、天の川の水や、三角点の青じろい微光の中を、どこまでもどこまでもと、走って行くのでした。

elated 大喜びの
hydrogen 「水素」
luminescent 発光性の
chugging and
clanking ガタゴトガタンゴトと音を立てながら

"Oh, gentians are blooming. It's autumn for sure," said Campanella, pointing out the window.

Magnificent purple gentians, so fine that they might have been carved out of moonstone, grew among the closely cropped grass that lined the track.

"Just you watch me hop right out of here, get some of those flowers and jump back on again," said Giovanni, his heart leaping with excitement.

"Too late," said Campanella. "We've left them behind now."

But no sooner had the words left his lips than had another batch of gentians flashed brightly past them, and then another, and another, cups with yellow at their hearts, gushing, passing in front of their eyes like rainfall … and a row of triangular turrets, some smoky, others burning, rose up, radiant for all the world to see.

THE NORTHERN CROSS AND PLIOCENE COAST

"I wonder if my mum will ever forgive me," said Campanella suddenly, stammering and flurried, but nonetheless resolute.

Giovanni was lost in his thoughts …

Sure, that's it! My mum is far down there by the orange-colored turret that looks like a speck of dust. She's thinking about me this instant.

"I'd go to the ends of the earth to make my mum happy," said Campanella, doing his best to hold back the tears. "But I just can't figure out what would make her happiest."

「ああ、りんどうの花が咲いている。もうすっかり秋だねえ。」カムパネルラが、窓の外を指さして言いました。

線路のへりになったみじかい芝草の中に、月長石ででも刻まれたような、すばらしい紫のりんどうの花が咲いていました。

「ぼく、飛び下りて、あいつをとって、また飛び乗ってみせようか。」ジョバンニは胸を躍らせて言いました。

「もうだめだ。あんなにうしろへ行ってしまったから。」

カムパネルラが、そう言ってしまうかしまわないうち、次のりんどうの花が、いっぱいに光って過ぎて行きました。

と思ったら、もう次から次から、たくさんのきいろな底をもったりんどうの花のコップが、湧くように、雨のように、眼の前を通り、三角標の列は、けむるように燃えるように、いよいよ光って立ったのです。

七、北十字とプリオシン海岸

「おっかさんは、ぼくをゆるして下さるだろうか。」

いきなり、カムパネルラが、思い切ったというように、少しどもりながら、急きこんで言いました。

ジョバンニは、

（ああ、そうだ、ぼくのおっかさんは、あの遠い一つのちりのように見える橙いろの三角標のあたりにいらっしゃって、いまぼくのことを考えているんだった。）と思いながら、ぼんやりしてだまっていました。

「ぼくはおっかさんが、ほんとうに幸になるなら、どんなことでもする。けれども、いったいどんなことが、おっかさんのいちばんの幸なんだろう。」カムパネルラは、なんだか、泣きだしたいのを、一生けん命こらえているようでした。

gentians 「りんどう」

carved out 「刻まれた」

moonstone 「月長石」。長石の一種で、結晶表面に光を当てると青色や白色に光る。この光の反射が月の輝きに似ているため、月長石と呼ばれる

gushing あふれ出る、わき出る

NORTHERN CROSS 「北十字」

PLIOCENE COAST 「プリオシン海岸」。Pliocene（鮮新世）とは、地質時代のひとつであり、500万年前から258万年前までの時代

stammering 「どもりながら」、口ごもって

flurried 「急きこんで」、慌てて、気が動転して

resolute 毅然とした、固く決心した

"At least there's nothing at all wrong with your mum," exclaimed Giovanni, somewhat taken aback.

"Oh, I dunno. It's just that, I mean, people create happiness when they do something good. That's why I'm sure my mum will forgive me."

Campanella looked like he had really made up his mind about something.

All at once, the inside of the wagon was flooded with a bright white light. Outside, where the water was flowing without sound or shape over the bed of the glittering river as if diamonds and dew from the grass had congealed on it, there was an island bathed in an aura of pale light. Atop the island, on a plateau, stood a cross, silent and eternal, so dazzling and white that it might have been cast from frozen Arctic clouds, crowned with a pure halo of gold.

"Hallelujah! Hallelujah!"

Voices came from the front and back. The two boys looked around to see passengers in the wagon, the folds of their robes hanging down perfectly straight, some clutching black Bibles to their chest, others with crystal rosaries around their neck, clasping their hands in prayer, all facing the cross outside.

Both boys found themselves rising to their feet. Campanella's cheeks gleamed like ripe apples.

The island and the cross moved gradually back down the line. The far bank of the Milky Way glowed through the mist, the pampas grass fluttered as if someone was breathing on it, the silver air was momentarily opaque with smoke, and the countless gentians vanished in the grass then reappeared like gentle will-o'-the-wisps.

「きみのおっかさんは、なんにもひどいことないじゃないの。」ジョバンニはびっくりして叫びました。

「ぼくわからない。けれども、誰だって、ほんとうにいいことをしたら、いちばん幸なんだねえ。だから、おっかさんは、ぼくをゆるして下さると思う。」カムパネルラは、なにかほんとうに決心しているように見えました。

俄かに、車のなかが、ぱっと白く明るくなりました。見ると、もうじつに、金剛石や草の露やあらゆる立派さをあつめたような、きらびやかな銀河の河床の上を水は声もなくかたちもなく流れ、その流れのまん中に、ぼうっと青白く後光の射した一つの島が見えるのでした。その島の平らないただきに、立派な眼もさめるような、白い十字架がたって、それはもう凍った北極の雲で鋳たといったらいいか、すきっとした金いろの円光をいただいて、しずかに永久に立っているのでした。

「ハルレヤ、ハルレヤ。」前からもうしろからも声が起りました。ふりかえって見ると、車室の中の旅人たちは、みなまっすぐにきもののひだを垂れ、黒いバイブルを胸にあてたり、水晶の珠数をかけたり、どの人もつつましく指を組み合せて、そっちに祈っているのでした。思わず二人もまっすぐに立ちあがりました。カムパネルラの頬は、まるで熟した苹果のあかしのようにうつくしくかがやいて見えました。

そして島と十字架とは、だんだんうしろの方へうつって行きました。

向う岸も、青じろくぽうっと光ってけむり、時々、やっぱりすすきが風にひるがえるらしく、さっとその銀いろがけむって、息でもかけたように見え、また、たくさんのりんどうの花が、草をかくれたり出たりするのは、やさしい狐火のように思われました。

taken aback 「びっくりして」

congealed 固まった、凝固した、凍った

halo 「円光」、後光

rosaries 「数珠」

clasping their hands 「指を組み合せて」

opaque くすんだ、不明瞭な

will-o'-the-wisps 「狐火」

But it wasn't long before clusters of pampas grass eclipsed the space between the river and the train, and they caught glimpses of Swan Island now far back in the distance, like a little picture, until the pampas grass rustled and swished once again, and the island disappeared entirely from view.

Behind Giovanni stood a tall Catholic nun he had not seen come on the train. She was dressed in black, and her perfectly round green eyes stared downward as she appeared to be listening humbly to a voice or words coming from the outside. The passengers returned to their seats in silence, while the two boys quietly exchanged words in a sad mood they had not felt before.

"We'll be at Swan Station any minute now, I guess."

"Yeah, we'll pull in at eleven o'clock on the button."

Before long, green signals and milky-white posts were flashing by the window, the dark lights of automatic switches, glowing indistinctly like sulfurous flames, passed on back, and the train gradually eased its pace, as a row of electric lights, perfectly spaced, appeared on a platform. The space between the lights became larger and larger, and the two boys came to a stop directly in front of the huge clock at Swan Station.

Two hands of blue tempered steel pointed precisely to eleven on the bracing autumn face of the clock. All the other passengers alighted together, leaving the wagon deserted.

A sign below the clock read ...

TWENTY MINUTE STOPOVER

"Should we get off here too?" asked Giovanni.

"Yeah, let's!"

それもほんのちょっとの間、川と汽車との間は、すすきの列でさえぎられ、白鳥の島は、二度ばかり、うしろの方に見えましたが、じきもうずうっと遠く小さく、絵のようになってしまい、またすすきがざわざわ鳴って、とうとうすっかり見えなくなってしまいました。

　ジョバンニのうしろには、いつから乗っていたのか、せいの高い、黒いかつぎをしたカトリック風の尼さんが、まん円な緑の瞳を、じっとまっすぐに落して、まだ何かことばか声かが、そっちから伝わって来るのを、虔んで聞いているというように見えました。旅人たちはしずかに席に戻り、二人も胸いっぱいのかなしみに似た新らしい気持ちを、何気なくちがった語で、そっと談し合ったのです。

　「もうじき白鳥の停車場だねえ。」

　「ああ、十一時かっきりには着くんだよ。」

　早くも、シグナルの緑の燈と、ぼんやり白い柱とが、ちらっと窓のそとを過ぎ、それから硫黄のほのおのようなくらいぼんやりした転てつ機の前のあかりが窓の下を通り、汽車はだんだんゆるやかになって、間もなくプラットホームの一列の電燈が、うつくしく規則正しくあらわれ、それがだんだん大きくなってひろがって、二人は丁度白鳥停車場の、大きな時計の前に来てとまりました。

　さわやかな秋の時計の盤面には、青く灼かれたはがねの二本の針が、くっきり十一時を指しました。みんなは、一ぺんに下りて、車室の中はがらんとなってしまいました。

　〔二十分停車〕と時計の下に書いてありました。

　「ぼくたちも降りて見ようか。」ジョバンニが言いました。

　「降りよう。」

eclipsed　覆い隠した

nun　尼僧、修道女

humbly　「虔んで」

pull in　（列車が）駅に到着する

automatic switches　「転てつ機」。列車を他のレール上に分岐させるための装置

sulfurous　「硫黄の」

bracing　「さわやかな」、すがすがしい

The two sprang up at once, flew out the door and made a mad dash for the ticket gate. But all they found at the gate was a bright purple electric light. There wasn't a soul around, not even a stationmaster or someone who resembled a redcap.

The boys came out onto a small square enclosed by gingko trees that looked hand carved of quartz. A wide road led from the square straight off into the bluish light of the Milky Way.

The people from the train seemed to have gone somewhere and vanished. Giovanni and Campanella started up the white road, shoulder to shoulder, casting shadows in all directions like two pillars in a room with windows on all sides or like the spokes of a wheel. Before they knew it they had reached the beautiful riverbed that they had seen from the train.

Campanella put a handful of sand into his palm and grated it with his fingers.

"This sand is all made up of crystals," he said as if in a dream. "There's a tiny fire burning inside each and every grain."

"Yeah!" exclaimed Giovanni, fairly sure that he had learned that somewhere.

All of the small stones on the bed were transparent, no doubt made up of quartz or topaz, some of them crumpled and folded in on themselves, others of corundum giving off a pale misty light from their facets. Giovanni ran straight for the water's edge and dipped his hand into the liquid. The mysterious water of the Milky Way was even clearer than hydrogen and the boys were convinced that it was flowing, because when their wrists were submerged in it they appeared to be floating as if in mercury, and the phosphorescent waves frothed and sparkled as they splashed against their skin.

二人は一度にはねあがってドアを飛び出して改札口へかけて行きました。ところが改札口には、明るい紫がかった電燈が、一つ点（つ）いているばかり、誰も居ませんでした。そこら中を見ても、駅長や赤帽らしい人の、影もなかったのです。

二人は、停車場の前の、水晶細工のように見える銀杏（いちょう）の木に囲まれた、小さな広場に出ました。そこから幅の広いみちが、まっすぐに銀河の青光の中へ通っていました。

さきに降りた人たちは、もうどこへ行ったか一人も見えませんでした。二人がその白い道を、肩をならべて行きますと、二人の影は、ちょうど四方に窓のある室（へや）の中の、二本の柱の影のように、また二つの車輪の輻（や）のように幾本も幾本も四方へ出るのでした。そして間もなく、あの汽車から見えたきれいな河原に来ました。

カムパネルラは、そのきれいな砂を一つまみ、掌（てのひら）にひろげ、指できしきしさせながら、夢のように言っているのでした。

「この砂はみんな水晶だ。中で小さな火が燃えている。」

「そうだ。」どこでぼくは、そんなこと習ったろうと思いながら、ジョバンニもぼんやり答えていました。

河原の礫（こいし）は、みんなすきとおって、たしかに水晶や黄玉や、またくしゃくしゃの皺曲（しゅうきょく）をあらわしたのや、また稜（かど）から霧のような青白い光を出す鋼玉やらでした。ジョバンニは、走ってその渚（なぎさ）に行って、水に手をひたしました。けれどもあやしいその銀河の水は、水素よりももっとすきとおっていたのです。それでもたしかに流れていたことは、二人の手首の、水にひたったとこが、少し水銀いろに浮いたように見え、その手首にぶっつかってできた波は、うつくしい燐光（りんこう）をあげて、ちらちらと燃えるように見えたのでもわかりました。

stationmaster 「駅長」

redcap 「赤帽」。鉄道駅構内で旅客の手荷物などを客の代わりに運搬する職業

gingko trees 「銀杏の木」

quartz 石英。透明な結晶は水晶となる

grated すりつぶした

crumpled 「くしゃくしゃの」

corundum 「鋼玉」。酸化アルミニウムの結晶で、色がついて美しいものはルビーやサファイヤなどの宝石となる

facets 小平面

submerged 「ひたった」、水中に沈んだ

mercury 「水銀」

frothed 泡立った

銀河鉄道の夜　59

Upstream, below a cliff that was blanketed in pampas grass, they caught sight of a stretch of white rock, as flat as a sports ground, following the course of the river. They could see the small figures of a number of people who seemed to be excavating or burying something as they stood up and stooped down with some sort of tool glinting from time to time in their hands.

"Let's go take a look," said the two boys nearly in unison as they ran for the cliff.

A shiny smooth ceramic nameplate stood at the entrance to the area of white rock ...

THE PLIOCENE COAST

Slim iron handrails had been planted in spots on the opposite bank, with lovely wooden benches sitting by them in the sand.

"Hey, I found something weird," said Campanella puzzled, stopping to pick up what looked like a long narrow black walnut with pointy ends.

"It's a walnut! Look, they're all over the place, probably carried along by the river. They're in the rock too!"

"They're big for walnuts. This one's twice as big as normal. And this one's in perfect shape."

"Let's go over where the people are right now. I bet they're digging up something or other."

The two boys went ahead holding their jaggedy black walnuts. To their left the ripples glowed against the water's edge like dim lightning, while to their right tufts of pampas grass, as if fashioned of silver or mother-of-pearl, blanketed the cliff face, swaying and rolling.

川上の方を見ると、すすきのいっぱいに生えている崖（がけ）の下に、白い岩が、まるで運動場のように平らに川に沿って出ているのでした。そこに小さな五六人の人かげが、何か掘り出すか埋めるかしているらしく、立ったり屈（かが）んだり、時々なにかの道具が、ピカッと光ったりしました。

　「行ってみよう。」二人は、まるで一度に叫んで、そっちの方へ走りました。その白い岩になった処（ところ）の入口に、

　［プリオシン海岸］という、瀬戸物のつるつるした標札が立って、向うの渚には、ところどころ、細い鉄の欄干も植えられ、木製のきれいなベンチも置いてありました。

　「おや、変なものがあるよ。」カムパネルラが、不思議そうに立ちどまって、岩から黒い細長いさきの尖（とが）ったくるみの実のようなものをひろいました。

　「くるみの実だよ。そら、沢山ある。流れて来たんじゃない。岩の中に入ってるんだ。」

　「大きいね、このくるみ、倍あるね。こいつはすこしもいたんでない。」

　「早くあすこへ行って見よう。きっと何か掘ってるから。」

　二人は、ぎざぎざの黒いくるみの実を持ちながら、またさっきの方へ近よって行きました。左手の渚（なぎさ）には、波がやさしい稲妻のように燃えて寄せ、右手の崖（がけ）には、いちめん銀や貝殻でこさえたようなすすきの穂がゆれたのです。

stooped down 「屈んだ」、身をかがめた

glinting 「ピカッと光った」

in unison 同時に、声をそろえて

walnut 「くるみの実」

jaggedy 「ぎざぎざの」

tufts of pampas grass 「すすきの穂」（tufts: ふさ、束）

fashioned こしらえた、作った

mother-of-pearl 真珠層

Once close enough to get a good look, they saw a tall scholarly man in boots and terribly thick glasses writing busily in a notebook. He was quite beside himself giving instructions to three assistants who were swinging pickaxes or shoveling with scoops.

"Don't break up that protuberance, use a scoop, a scoop! Watch out, dig around it first. No, not that way! No, no, go easy with it, will ya?"

The massive pale skeleton of a beast protruded from the soft white rock. A good half of it had already been excavated. It was crushed on its side. The rock itself, which bore two cloven hoof prints, had been carefully carved out into some ten numbered squares.

"You fellows here to inspect?" asked the scholarly man, twinkling his glasses. "You saw all those walnuts, didn't you? They'd be somewhere in the neighborhood of, oh, 1,200,000 years old, I'd say. Not very old, when you come down to it. This place here was a coastline some 1,200,000 years back, just about after the Tertiary Period. Plenty of shells under here too. Saltwater ebbed and flowed here where the river is now. Now, take this beast here. We geologists call it a 'bos' ... hey, you, put down that pick! Can't you be more careful and use a chisel? This bos was the ancestor of today's cow. This place, I'd say, would've been literally crawling with them."

"Are you going to make a specimen out of it?"

だんだん近付いて見ると、一人のせいの高い、ひどい近眼鏡をかけ、長靴をはいた学者らしい人が、手帳に何かせわしそうに書きつけながら、鶴嘴をふりあげたり、スコープをつかったりしている、三人の助手らしい人たちに夢中でいろいろ指図をしていました。

「そこのその突起を壊さないように。スコープを使いたまえ、スコープを。おっと、も少し遠くから掘って。いけない、いけない。なぜそんな乱暴をするんだ。」

見ると、その白い柔らかな岩の中から、大きな大きな青じろい獣の骨が、横に倒れて潰れたという風になって、半分以上掘り出されていました。そして気をつけて見ると、そこらには、蹄の二つある足跡のついた岩が、四角に十ばかり、きれいに切り取られて番号がつけられてありました。

「君たちは参観かね。」その大学士らしい人が、眼鏡をきらっとさせて、こっちを見て話しかけました。

「くるみが沢山あったろう。それはまあ、ざっと百二十万年ぐらい前のくるみだよ。ごく新らしい方さ。ここは百二十万年前、第三紀のあとのころは海岸でね、この下からは貝がらも出る。いま川の流れているとこに、そっくり塩水が寄せたり引いたりもしていたのだ。このけものかね、これはボスといってね、おいおい、そこつるはしはよしたまえ。ていねいに鑿でやってくれたまえ。ボスといってね、いまの牛の先祖で、昔はたくさん居たさ。」

「標本にするんですか。」

pickaxes 「鶴嘴」

protuberance 「突起」

protruded 飛び出した

cloven hoof 割れた蹄

Tertiary Period 「第三紀」。地質時代の旧区分のひとつで、およそ6600万年前から258万年前までの時代

ebbed and flowed 「寄せたり引いたり」、満ち引きした

geologist 地質学者

bos ウシ科ウシ属のラテン名。特に、Bos primigenius（ボス・プリミゲニウス）は牛の祖先といわれる。

chisel 「鑿」

specimen 「標本」

"No, we need this as evidence. You see, we know this place to be a magnificent thick stratum, and we've got all the proof we need that it was formed 1,200,000 years ago. But some others don't see it in that light, claiming that it might be just wind, water or empty sky. Follow? However ... hey, you, don't use your scoop on that! There's bound to be a set of ribs buried under there."

The professor scurried over to the dig.

"It's time," said Campanella, checking his wristwatch with the map. "Let's go."

"Well, I am afraid that we must take our leave," said Giovanni, bowing formally to the professor.

"Must you? Well, goodbye then," he said, rushing helter-skelter about and supervising things right and left.

As for the boys, they ran for their lives back over the white rock so as not to miss the train. They found themselves running just like the wind without skipping a single breath or getting hot sore knees.

If we can run like this, we can run anywhere in the whole wide world!

That's what Giovanni thought as they passed by the river bed. The light on the ticket gate gradually grew larger and larger, and, in a flash, they were back in their old seats looking out the window at the very place they had been not a moment ago.

THE BIRDCATCHER

"Mind if I sit down here?"

Giovanni and Campanella heard a kindly, gravelly adult's voice behind them.

「いや、証明するに要るんだ。ぼくらからみると、ここは厚い立派な地層で、百二十万年ぐらい前にできたという証拠もいろいろあがるけれども、ぼくらとちがったやつからみてもやっぱりこんな地層に見えるかどうか、あるいは風か水やがらんとした空かに見えやしないかということなのだ。わかったかい。けれども、おいおい。そこもスコープではいけない。そのすぐ下に肋骨が埋もれてる筈じゃないか。」大学士はあわてて走って行きました。

「もう時間だよ。行こう。」カムパネルラが地図と腕時計とをくらべながら言いました。

「ああ、ではわたくしどもは失礼いたします。」ジョバンニは、ていねいに大学士におじぎしました。

「そうですか。いや、さよなら。」大学士は、また忙がしそうに、あちこち歩きまわって監督をはじめました。二人は、その白い岩の上を、一生けん命汽車におくれないように走りました。そしてほんとうに、風のように走れたのです。息も切れず膝もあつくなりませんでした。

こんなにしてかけるなら、もう世界中だってかけれると、ジョバンニは思いました。

そして二人は、前のあの河原を通り、改札口の電燈がだんだん大きくなって、間もなく二人は、もとの車室の席に座って、いま行って来た方を、窓から見ていました。

八、鳥を捕る人

「ここへかけてもようございますか。」

がさがさした、けれども親切そうな、大人の声が、二人のうしろで聞えました。

stratum 「地層」

bound to be... 〜にちがいない、〜する運命にある

scurried 「あわてて走って」

helter-skelter 「あちこち」、慌てふためいて、行き当たりばったりに

in a flash 「間もなく」、すぐに、一瞬で

gravelly 「がさがさした」、（声が）がらがらの、しわがれた

The voice had come from a man with a stoop and a red beard, dressed in a shaggy brown overcoat and carrying a huge bundle wrapped in white cloth and slung in two equal halves over his shoulders.

"Fine with us," said Giovanni in reply, shrugging.

The man smiled faintly through his beard and lifted his bundle carefully onto the baggage rack above.

Giovanni was feeling immensely sad and lonely as he stared in silence at the clock in front of him. Far up ahead what sounded like a glass flute rang out and the train moved smoothly forward. Campanella was examining the ceiling. A black beetle had come to rest on one of the lights, casting a monstrous shadow. The man with the red beard was staring intently at the two boys and smiling, as if something was taking him back to somewhere or some time else. The train gradually began to pick up speed, and the pampas grass and river alternated in lighting up the air outside.

"May I enquire as to where you boys would be heading?" asked the man timidly.

"Further than anybody," answered Giovanni sheepishly.

"That's really something. That's precisely where this train is going."

"So where are you going?" asked Campanella suddenly in a quarreling tone that made Giovanni smile.

Then a man across the aisle, sporting a pointy cap and dangling a large key from his waist, stole a look at them and smiled too, making Campanella blush and smile himself. But the man with the red beard didn't look angry in the least.

それは、茶いろの少しぼろぼろの外套を着て、白い巾でつつんだ荷物を、二つに分けて肩に掛けた、赤髯のせなかのかがんだ人でした。

　「ええ、いいんです。」ジョバンニは、少し肩をすぼめて挨拶しました。その人は、ひげの中でかすかに微笑いながら荷物をゆっくり網棚にのせました。

　ジョバンニは、なにか大へんさびしいようなかなしいような気がして、だまって正面の時計を見ていましたら、ずうっと前の方で、硝子の笛のようなものが鳴りました。汽車はもう、しずかにうごいていたのです。カムパネルラは、車室の天井を、あちこち見ていました。その一つのあかりに黒い甲虫がとまってその影が大きく天井にうつっていたのです。赤ひげの人は、なにかなつかしそうにわらいながら、ジョバンニやカムパネルラのようすを見ていました。汽車はもうだんだん早くなって、すすきと川と、かわるがわる窓の外から光りました。

　赤ひげの人が、少しおずおずしながら、二人に訊きました。

　「あなた方は、どちらへいらっしゃるんですか。」

　「どこまでも行くんです。」ジョバンニは、少しきまり悪そうに答えました。

　「それはいいね。この汽車は、じっさい、どこまででも行きますぜ。」

　「あなたはどこへ行くんです。」カムパネルラが、いきなり、喧嘩のようにたずねましたので、ジョバンニは、思わずわらいました。すると、向うの席に居た、尖った帽子をかぶり、大きな鍵を腰に下げた人も、ちらっとこっちを見てわらいましたので、カムパネルラも、つい顔を赤くして笑いだしてしまいました。ところがその人は別に怒ったでもなく、頬をぴくぴくしながら返事しました。

shaggy　もじゃもじゃの、けば立った、粗野な

slung... over his shoulders　〜を「肩に掛けた」

staring intently at...　〜をじっと見ている、まじまじと見ている

enquire　尋ねる、聞く

timidly　「おずおずしながら」、おそるおそる

sheepishly　「きまり悪そうに」

sporting　見せびらかす

dangling　ぶら下げる

銀河鉄道の夜　67

"I'm gettin' off a bit down the track," he said with his cheeks twitching. "Birdcatchin's my line."

"What birds do you catch?"

"Why, cranes an' wild geese. An' herons an' swans, too."

"Are there lots of cranes here?"

"Masses. They were just yelpin' back there, didn't ya hear 'em?"

"No."

"If ya listen you can still hear 'em now. Prick up your ears and listen."

Giovanni and Campanella raised their eyes and listened carefully. Amidst the soft echo of the chugging of the train and the swishing of the pampas grass they heard the bubbly frothing and gurgling of water.

"How do you catch a crane?"

"Do you mean cranes or herons?"

"Uh, herons," said Giovanni, not really caring which.

"Easy as pie! Herons are made of congealed sand from the Milky Way's bed, an' they keep comin' back to the river in a constant stream. If you wait on the bank all of them come soarin' down with their feet out like this, an' I pluck 'em off like sittin' ducks just before they reach the ground. Then they curdle up and pass on serenely to, well, greener pastures. Everybody knows what happens next. You press 'em."

"Press 'em? You mean like flowers or specimens?"

"They're not specimens, no. I mean, everybody eats 'em. You boys know that much, don't you?"

"Sounds funny to me," said Campanella, cocking his head.

「わっしはすぐそこで降ります。わっしは、鳥をつかまえる商売でね。」

「何鳥ですか。」

「鶴(つる)や雁(がん)です。さぎも白鳥もです。」

「鶴はたくさんいますか。」

「居ますとも、さっきから鳴いてまさあ。聞かなかったのですか。」

「いいえ。」

「いまでも聞えるじゃありませんか。そら、耳をすまして聴いてごらんなさい。」

　二人は眼を挙げ、耳をすましました。ごとごと鳴る汽車のひびきと、すすきの風との間から、ころんころんと水の湧(わ)くような音が聞えて来るのでした。

「鶴、どうしてとるんですか。」

「鶴ですか、それとも鷺(さぎ)ですか。」

「鷺です。」ジョバンニは、どっちでもいいと思いながら答えました。

「そいつはな、雑作(ぞうさ)ない。さぎというものは、みんな天の川の砂が凝(こご)って、ぼおっとできるもんですからね、そして始終川へ帰りますからね、川原で待っていて、鷺(さぎ)がみんな、脚をこういう風にして下りてくるとこを、そいつが地べたへつくかつかないうちに、ぴたっと押えちまうんです。するともう鷺は、かたまって安心して死んじまいます。あとはもう、わかり切ってまさあ。押し葉にするだけです。」

「鷺を押し葉にするんですか。標本ですか。」

「標本じゃありません。みんなたべるじゃありませんか。」

「おかしいねえ。」カムパネルラが首をかしげました。

down the track　後で、将来

twitching　ぴくぴく動く、引きつる

geese　「雁」、ガチョウ

herons　「さぎ」

curdle up　「かたまって」、凍り付かせる

serenely　「安心して」、落ち着いて、穏やかに

greener pastures　よりよい場所

cocking his head　「首をかしげました」

"Good heavens, it ain't funny an' it ain't dubious in the least. Watch." The man stood up and brought his bundle down from the rack, untying it with a nimble twirl of his fingers.

"Feast your eyes! A fresh batch."

"They really are herons!" blurted out the boys.

There were some ten of them, somewhat flattened down, their black legs crumpled in under them, lying in a row side by side as if carved in relief, their pure white bodies radiating the very light of the Northern Cross that they had passed.

"They've all got their eyes closed," said Campanella, gently touching a bird's white eyelid that was the shape of a crescent moon. They even had white feathers like spears on their heads.

"See what I mean?" said the birdcatcher, wrapping up his catch again, folding the cloth and securing it with twine.

Who on earth around here would eat a heron?

This is what Giovanni thought as he asked, "Do herons taste good?"

"Good as goose! I've got orders flyin' in faster than I can fill 'em. But the wild geese, I should say, are in greater demand. Geese have much more breeding, an' what's more, they cause no trouble in the handling. Here."

The birdcatcher untied the other bundle. Inside it was a row of yellow, off-white and speckled geese with their beaks lined up neatly and their bodies slightly flattened out, just like the herons.

"These geese may be gobbled anytime. How about it? Dig in."

The birdcatcher gently pulled the yellow leg of a goose. It came off in a nice clean piece, as if made of chocolate.

「おかしいも不審もありませんや。そら。」その男は立って、網棚から包みをおろして、手ばやくくるくると解きました。

「さあ、ごらんなさい。いまとって来たばかりです。」

「ほんとうに鷺だねえ。」二人は思わず叫びました。まっ白な、あのさっきの北の十字架のように光る鷺のからだが、十ばかり、少しひらべったくなって、黒い脚をちぢめて、浮彫のようにならんでいたのです。

「眼をつぶってるね。」カムパネルラは、指でそっと、鷺の三日月がたの白い瞑った眼にさわりました。頭の上の槍のような白い毛もちゃんとついていました。

「ね、そうでしょう。」鳥捕りは風呂敷を重ねて、またくるくると包んで紐でくくりました。誰がいったいここらで鷺なんぞ喰べるだろうとジョバンニは思いながら訊きました。

「鷺はおいしいんですか。」

「ええ、毎日注文があります。しかし雁の方が、もっと売れます。雁の方がずっと柄がいいし、第一手数がありませんからな。そら。」鳥捕りは、また別の方の包みを解きました。すると黄と青じろとまだらになって、なにかのあかりのようにひかる雁が、ちょうどさっきの鷺のように、くちばしを揃えて、少し扁べったくなって、ならんでいました。

「こっちはすぐ喰べられます。どうです、少しおあがりなさい。」鳥捕りは、黄いろな雁の足を、軽くひっぱりました。するとそれは、チョコレートででもできているように、すっときれいにはなれました。

dubious　不審な、疑わしい

nimble　すばやい

batch　ひとまとまりの数量

blurted out　うっかり口走った

crumpled　つぶされて、ねじれて

spears　「槍」

twine　より糸、麻ひも

speckled　まだらの

These geese may be gobbled　these と geese は韻を踏んでいる。gobble には「ガツガツ食べる」の意味の他に七面鳥の鳴き声の意味があるため、gobble を擬声語として用いて語呂合わせをしている

Dig in.　「おあがりなさい」

"Eh, how about it? Have a piece on me," he said, breaking the leg in two and giving them a half each.

Giovanni took a little bite and thought to himself ...

Hold on, this is cake! It even tastes better than chocolate. This man is pulling our leg when he says that these geese can fly. He's just a cake salesman out in the field somewhere. But I do feel sorry for him, taking his cake and eating it too.

But even so, he didn't stop munching away.

"Have another bite," said the birdcatcher, reaching again for his bundle.

"Thank you just the same," declined Giovanni, who really did want to have another piece.

So the birdcatcher offered it to the man with the large key in the seat across the aisle from him.

"Much obliged, but I shouldn't really be dippin' into your stock," said the man, tipping his cap.

"Don't mention it," said the birdcatcher, adding, "Well, how're things goin' in the world of migratory birds?"

"Great, we're runnin' at full capacity. Just day before yesterday, during the second shift, calls kept comin' in askin' me why the light in the lighthouse was on the blink, blinkin' at irregular intervals, you know, so I says to 'em, heaven only knows, it's not my doin', but it's the birds migratin' in big packed flocks passin' in front of the light, so what can you do? Ain't no good come complainin' to me, I tell 'em, take your complaint, I says, to the big fella with the long narrow beak an' the spindly legs, the one wearin' the cape that flutters in the wind! I gave it to 'em, I did! Ha!"

The pampas grass was gone now leaving the field outside shining with a new radiance.

「どうです。すこしたべてごらんなさい。」鳥捕りは、それを二つにちぎってわたしました。ジョバンニは、ちょっと喰べてみて、（なんだ、やっぱりこいつはお菓子だ。チョコレートよりも、もっとおいしいけれども、こんな雁が飛んでいるもんか。この男は、どこかそこらの野原の菓子屋だ。けれどもぼくは、このひとをばかにしながら、この人のお菓子をたべているのは、大へん気の毒だ。）とおもいながら、やっぱりぽくぽくそれをたべていました。

「も少しおあがりなさい。」鳥捕りがまた包みを出しました。ジョバンニは、もっとたべたかったのですけれども、

「ええ、ありがとう。」と言って遠慮しましたら、鳥捕りは、こんどは向うの席の、鍵（かぎ）をもった人に出しました。

「いや、商売ものを貰（もら）っちゃすみませんな。」その人は、帽子をとりました。

「いいえ、どういたしまして。どうです、今年の渡り鳥の景気は。」

「いや、すてきなもんですよ。一昨日（おととい）の第二限ころなんか、なぜ燈台の灯を、規則以外に間〔一字分空白〕させるかって、あっちからもこっちからも、電話で故障が来ましたが、なあに、こっちがやるんじゃなくて、渡り鳥どもが、まっ黒にかたまって、あかしの前を通るのですから仕方ありませんや。わたしゃ、べらぼうめ、そんな苦情は、おれのとこへ持って来たって仕方がねえや、ばさばさのマントを着て脚と口との途方もなく細い大将へやれって、こう言ってやりましたがね、はっは。」

すすきがなくなったために、向うの野原から、ぱっとあかりが射（さ）して来ました。

pulling our leg　自分たちをからかう、鳥捕りが鳥の足を引っ張ることとかけている。

taking his cake and eating it too　いいとこ取りをする、食い物にしている

Much obliged　「ありがとう」

tipping　（帽子を）軽く持ち上げる

migratory birds　「渡り鳥」

fella　「大将」、男

spindly　「細い」、ひょろっとした

銀河鉄道の夜　73

"What makes the herons so hard to handle?" Campanella had been meaning to ask this from before.

"Look," said the birdcatcher, turning back to the boys, "you see, if you want to eat a heron, you've gotta first hang him up for a good ten days in the liquid light of the Milky Way, or you can bury 'em in the sand for a few days. It evaporates the mercury and then you can eat 'em."

"This is no bird, it's really cake, isn't it!"

Both Giovanni and Campanella had been thinking this, but it was Campanella who had taken the plunge and come out with it.

"That's right, this is where I get off," said the birdcatcher, looking in a frightful tizzy. He then stood up, grabbed his big cloth bundle and, in a flash, was nowhere to be seen.

The boys looked at each other, their eyes saying, "Where did he go?" But the lighthouse keeper was all grin, leaning in front of the boys to peer out their window.

Out there they all saw the very same birdcatcher who had been with them a moment before. He was standing on a riverbank surrounded by cudweed that was giving off a lovely yellow and eggshell-white phosphorescence. He was staring up at the sky with a determined look, his two arms stretched out like wings.

イラスト：ルーシー・バルバース

「鷺の方はなぜ手数なんですか。」カムパネルラは、さっきから、訊こうと思っていたのです。

「それはね、鷺を喰べるには、」鳥捕りは、こっちに向き直りました。

「天の川の水あかりに、十日もつるして置くかね、そうでなけぁ、砂に三四日うずめなけぁいけないんだ。そうすると、水銀がみんな蒸発して、喰べられるようになるよ。」

「こいつは鳥じゃない。ただのお菓子でしょう。」やっぱりおなじことを考えていたとみえて、カムパネルラが、思い切ったというように、尋ねました。鳥捕りは、何か大へんあわてた風で、

「そうそう、ここで降りなけぁ。」と言いながら、立って荷物をとったと思うと、もう見えなくなっていました。

「どこへ行ったんだろう。」

二人は顔を見合せましたら、燈台守は、にやにや笑って、少し伸びあがるようにしながら、二人の横の窓の外をのぞきました。二人もそっちを見ましたら、たったいまの鳥捕りが、黄いろと青じろの、うつくしい燐光を出す、いちめんのかわらははこぐさの上に立って、まじめな顔をして両手をひろげて、じっとそらを見ていたのです。

liquid light 「水あかり」
taken the plunge 「思い切った」
tizzy あわてた
cudweed 「ははこぐさ」
phosphorescence 「燐光」

"There he is! It's so weird. I bet he's got his eye on the birds right now. If only they would fly down before the train goes by!"

No sooner had those words left Giovanni's mouth than did a veritable snowfall of herons, squawking and calling, come fluttering down from the barren dark violet sky. At that, the birdcatcher, chuckling with glee that things were really coming his way now, spread out his legs on a sixty-degree angle, taking in the birds by their black legs hand over fist and pinning them down in his cloth bag. Once inside the bag the birds flickered blue, on and off like fireflies, until, in the end, they turned a hazy-white color and shut their eyes.

Most of the birds, however, were not caught. They came to a safe landing on top of the sand by the river, and as their feet touched the sand their bodies curled in, flattening like melted snow, spreading along the surface like molten copper fresh from a blast furnace, their forms clinging momentarily to the sand, turning light and dark, light and dark, until finally blending in without a trace.

The birdcatcher, now with some twenty birds in his bag, suddenly lifted both arms skyward, like a soldier who had been hit by a bullet and was on his last legs ... when, in a flash, there was no sign of him outside and Giovanni heard a familiar voice coming from the seat next to him.

"Ah, I feel like a new man. Yep, nothin' like a hard day's work, best way to earn a crust!"

It was the birdcatcher himself, making rows of the herons he had just caught and stacking them in neat piles.

veritable 「まるで」、紛れもない

squawking 「ぎゃあぎゃあ」

barren 「がらんとした」、不毛の

chuckling with glee 「ほくほくして」、ほくそ笑んで

molten copper 「銅の汁」、溶融銅

blast furnace 「熔鉱炉」

clinging まとわりつく

bullet 「鉄砲弾」、銃弾

on his last legs 死にかかって、疲れ切って、弱り果てて

earn a crust 「稼いでいる」、生計を立てる

「あすこへ行ってる。ずいぶん奇体だねえ。きっとまた鳥をつかまえるとこだねえ。汽車が走って行かないうちに、早く鳥がおりるといいな。」と言った途端、がらんとした桔梗いろの空から、さっき見たような鷺が、まるで雪の降るように、ぎゃあぎゃあ叫びながら、いっぱいに舞いおりて来ました。するとあの鳥捕りは、すっかり注文通りだというようにほくほくして、両足をかっきり六十度に開いて立って、鷺のちぢめて降りて来る黒い脚を両手で片っ端から押えて、布の袋の中に入れるのでした。すると鷺は、蛍のように、袋の中でしばらく、青くぺかぺか光ったり消えたりしていましたが、おしまいとうとう、みんなぼんやり白くなって、眼をつぶるのでした。ところが、つかまえられる鳥よりは、つかまえられないで無事に天の川の砂の上に降りるものの方が多かったのです。それは見ていると、足が砂へつくや否や、まるで雪の融けるように、縮まって扁べったくなって、間もなく熔鉱炉から出た銅の汁のように、砂や砂利の上にひろがり、しばらくは鳥の形が、砂についているのでしたが、それも二三度明るくなったり暗くなったりしているうちに、もうすっかりまわりと同じいろになってしまうのでした。

　鳥捕りは二十疋ばかり、袋に入れてしまうと、急に両手をあげて、兵隊が鉄砲弾にあたって、死ぬときのような形をしました。と思ったら、もうそこに鳥捕りの形はなくなって、却って、

「ああせいせいした。どうもからだに恰度合うほど稼いでいるくらい、いいことはありませんな。」というききおぼえのある声が、ジョバンニの隣りにしました。見ると鳥捕りは、もうそこでとって来た鷺を、きちんとそろえて、一つずつ重ね直しているのでした。

銀河鉄道の夜　77

"How did you get back here all at once?" asked Giovanni, feeling both that he had expected the man to do it and yet that it was something quite miraculous as well.

"How? 'Cause I wanted to, that's how. Now, where on earth was it you two boys said you hailed from?"

Giovanni was about to answer when he realized that he couldn't for the life of him recall where in the world he had come from. Campanella, too, had turned bright red trying to remember.

"Well, from a long, long way off, anyway," said the birdcatcher, nodding as if he knew all about it.

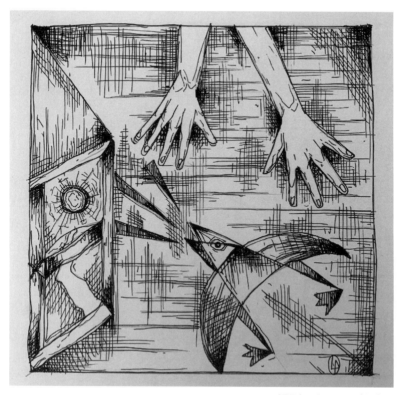

イラスト：ルーシー・バルバース

「どうしてあすこから、いっぺんにここへ来たんですか。」ジョバンニが、なんだかあたりまえのような、あたりまえでないような、おかしな気がして問いました。

「どうしてって、来ようとしたから来たんです。ぜんたいあなた方は、どちらからおいでですか。」

ジョバンニは、すぐ返事しようと思いましたけれども、さあ、ぜんたいどこから来たのか、もうどうしても考えつきませんでした。カムパネルラも、顔をまっ赤にして何か思い出そうとしているのでした。

「ああ、遠くからですね。」鳥捕りは、わかったというように雑作なくうなずきました。

hailed from...　〜の出身である

GIOVANNI'S TICKET

"We are about to leave Swan Zone. See for yourself. There's the renowned Albireo Observatory."

Outside the window, four big black buildings stood in the very middle of the Milky Way, which itself was a galaxy of fireworks. Two enormous spheres, of translucent blue sapphire and dazzling yellow topaz invisibly looped together, were revolving around each other on the flat roof of one of the buildings. When the yellow one made its way around back, the smaller blue one circled forward until their edges overlapped, forming a single, exquisite, green convex lens-like shape. Then gradually the center would bulge and the blue sapphire would appear exactly in front, a green sphere with a yellow topaz ring around it. Again, slowly, the sapphire would move across to the other edge, reversing the shape of the lens before, and the two would part company as the topaz came forward. The black observatory buildings lay there silently, as if at rest, encircled in the formless, soundless liquid of the Milky Way.

"That's an instrument for measuring the speed of the water as it flows. You see, the water ..."

That was all the birdcatcher could say before, without warning, a tall conductor in a red cap came up to their seats.

"Please have your tickets ready," he said.

The birdcatcher pulled a small slip of paper from his inside pocket without saying a word. The conductor glanced at it, immediately turning to Giovanni and Campanella, wagging his finger and pointing to them, as if to say, "And where are your tickets?"

九、ジョバンニの切符

「もうここらは白鳥区のおしまいです。ごらんなさい。あれが名高いアルビレオの観測所です。」

窓の外の、まるで花火でいっぱいのような、あまの川のまん中に、黒い大きな建物が四棟_{むね}ばかり立って、その一つの平屋根の上に、眼もさめるような、青宝玉^{サファイア}と黄玉^{トパース}の大きな二つのすきとおった球が、輪になってしずかにくるくるとまわっていました。黄いろのがだんだん向うへまわって行って、青い小さいのがこっちへ進んで来、間もなく二つのはじは、重なり合って、きれいな緑いろの両面凸_{とつ}レンズのかたちをつくり、それもだんだん、まん中がふくらみ出して、とうとう青いのは、すっかりトパースの正面に来ましたので、緑の中心と黄いろな明るい環_わとができました。それがまただんだん横へ外れて、前のレンズの形を逆に繰り返し、とうとうすっとはなれて、サファイアは向うへめぐり、黄いろのはこっちへ進み、また丁度さっきのような風になりました。銀河の、かたちもなく音もない水にかこまれて、ほんとうにその黒い測候所が、睡_{ねむ}っているように、しずかによこたわったのです。

「あれは、水の速さをはかる器械です。水も……。」鳥捕りが言いかけたとき、

「切符を拝見いたします。」三人の席の横に、赤い帽子をかぶったせいの高い車掌が、いつかまっすぐに立っていて言いました。鳥捕りは、だまってかくしから、小さな紙きれを出しました。車掌はちょっと見て、すぐ眼をそらして、（あなた方のは？）というように、指をうごかしながら、手をジョバンニたちの方へ出しました。

Observatory 「観測所」

exquisite 「きれいな」、非常に美しい

bulge 「ふくらみ出して」

encircled 「かこまれて」

wagging 「うごかしながら」、振りながら

"Oh, gee," said Giovanni, fidgeting at a loss for what to do. But Campanella produced a small gray ticket from out of nowhere, as if by second nature. Giovanni, now in a real flurry, reached deeply into his jacket pocket to see if there was a ticket there, finding a big folded piece of paper. He quickly brought out his hand, surprised himself that there was something in it, and held up a green piece of paper, folded in quarters, about the size of a postcard. He thought ...

I don't know what this paper is, but the conductor has his hand out, so I may as well hand it to him!

The conductor took the piece of paper from him, stood at attention and carefully unfolded it. He fiddled with the buttons on his jacket as he read it, while the lighthouse keeper did his best to steal a peek at it from below. Giovanni, quite excited, was sure that the paper was some kind of certificate.

"Have you carried this from the Third Spatial Region?" asked the conductor.

"Search me," said Giovanni, chuckling and looking up, now feeling considerably relieved and safe.

"Very well. We will be arriving at the Southern Cross in the neighborhood of the next Third Hour," said the conductor, returning Giovanni's ticket and proceeding on down the aisle.

Campanella was dying to find out what was written on Giovanni's ticket, so he quickly took a peek at it. Giovanni couldn't wait to see either. But all they could make out on it were designs of black arabesques with ten or so funny-looking printed letters among them. They felt that if they continued to stare at the piece of paper they would certainly be swallowed up into it.

　「さあ、」ジョバンニは困って、もじもじしていましたら、カムパネルラは、わけもないという風で、小さな鼠《ねずみ》いろの切符を出しました。ジョバンニは、すっかりあわててしまって、もしか上着のポケットにでも、入っていたかとおもいながら、手を入れて見ましたら、何か大きな畳んだ紙きれにあたりました。こんなもの入っていたろうかと思って、急いで出してみましたら、それは四つに折ったはがきぐらいの大きさの緑いろの紙でした。車掌が手を出しているもんですから何でも構わない、やっちまえと思って渡しましたら、車掌はまっすぐに立ち直って叮嚀にそれを開いて見ていました。そして読みながら上着のぼたんやなんかしきりに直したりしていましたし燈台看守も下からそれを熱心にのぞいていましたから、ジョバンニはたしかにあれは証明書か何かだったと考えて少し胸が熱くなるような気がしました。

　「これは三次空間の方からお持ちになったのですか。」車掌がたずねました。

　「何だかわかりません。」もう大丈夫だと安心しながらジョバンニはそっちを見あげてくつくつ笑いました。

　「よろしゅうございます。南十字《サウザンクロス》へ着きますのは、次の第三時ころになります。」車掌は紙をジョバンニに渡して向うへ行きました。

　カムパネルラは、その紙切れが何だったか待ち兼ねたというように急いでのぞきこみました。ジョバンニも全く早く見たかったのです。ところがそれはいちめん黒い唐草《からくさ》のような模様の中に、おかしな十ばかりの字を印刷したものでだまって見ていると何だかその中へ吸い込まれてしまうような気がするのでした。すると鳥捕りが横からちらっとそれを見てあわてたように言いました。

fidgeting 「もじもじして」、そわそわして

second nature 自然に、慣れた風に

in a flurry 「すっかり慌てて」、慌ただしく

fiddled with... 〜をいじくりまわした

Third Spatial Region 「三次空間」。地上の世界

"Search me" 「わかりません」

Third Hour 「第三時」

arabesques 唐草模様

"Good heavens," said the birdcatcher, taking a glimpse from the side. "That ticket is really tops. It will take you higher than the sky! Even higher. With this ticket you've got safe conduct to anywhere your heart desires to go. With this ticket you can go wherever you wish on the imperfect Four Dimensional Milky Way Dream Train. You boys are really something!"

"Oh, I dunno," said Giovanni, blushing, folding up his ticket and putting it back in his pocket.

He felt rather awkward as he stared out the window with Campanella, vaguely aware that the birdcatcher was throwing them glances from time to time, as if to say, "You boys are really tops!"

"We'll be pulling into Eagle Station any moment," said Campanella, comparing his map with three little pale-white triangular turrets on the opposite bank.

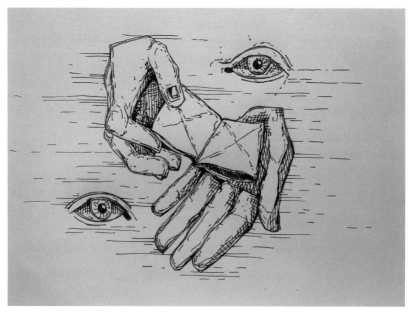

イラスト：ルーシー・パルバース

「おや、こいつは大したもんですぜ。こいつはもう、ほんとうの天上へさえ行ける切符だ。天上どこじゃない、どこでも勝手にあるける通行券です。こいつをお持ちになれぁ、なるほど、こんな不完全な幻想第四次の銀河鉄道なんか、どこまででも行ける筈でさあ、あなた方大したもんですね。」

「何だかわかりません。」ジョバンニが赤くなって答えながらそれをまた畳んでかくしに入れました。そしてきまりが悪いのでカムパネルラと二人、また窓の外をながめていましたが、その鳥捕りの時々大したもんだというようにちらちらこっちを見ているのがぼんやりわかりました。

「もうじき鷲の停車場だよ。」カムパネルラが向う岸の、三つならんだ小さな青じろい三角標と地図とを見較べて言いました。

Giovanni, without knowing why, felt indescribably sorry for the birdcatcher, and when he thought about him being so overjoyed at becoming a new man when he caught his herons, wrapping them up in his white cloth bundle or just stealing glances at people's tickets and praising them to the high heavens, he wanted to give him everything he owned, his food and everything, though he really didn't know him very well at all. If it would make the birdcatcher happy, he would even stand for a hundred years at a time in the shining field of the Milky Way and catch his birds for him.

Giovanni couldn't remain silent any longer. "What is it you wish for more than anything else?" is what he wanted to ask him. But that would be altogether too abrupt. As he considered what else he might ask and turned toward the birdcatcher ... the birdcatcher wasn't there at all! And his huge white bundle was gone from the overhead rack as well.

Giovanni immediately looked outside, sure that he would be out there, his legs planted solidly, searching the skies for a heron to catch. But his broad back and tapered hat were nowhere to be seen. All that was there was a waving white sea of pampas grass and a beautiful blanket of sand.

"Where'd he go off to?" asked Campanella in a daze.

"That's a good question. I wonder where on earth we'll ever meet up with him again. I just wanted to say a few more words to him."

"Oh, me too."

"I really feel awful, because at first I thought he was in our way."

Giovanni had never felt odd in quite that way and certainly had never been able to express it in words.

ジョバンニはなんだかわけもわからずににわかにとなりの鳥捕りが気の毒でたまらなくなりました。鷺をつかまえてせいせいしたとよろこんだり、白いきれでそれをくるくる包んだり、ひとの切符をびっくりしたように横目で見てあわててほめだしたり、そんなことを――考えていると、もうその見ず知らずの鳥捕りのために、ジョバンニの持っているものでも食べるものでもなんでもやってしまいたい、もうこの人のほんとうの幸になるなら自分があの光る天の川の河原に立って百年つづけて立って鳥をとってやってもいいというような気がして、どうしてももう黙っていられなくなりました。ほんとうにあなたのほしいものは一体何ですか、と訊こうとして、それではあんまり出し抜けだから、どうしようかと考えて振り返って見ましたら、そこにはもうあの鳥捕りが居ませんでした。網棚の上には白い荷物も見えなかったのです。また窓の外で足をふんばってそらを見上げて鷺を捕る支度をしているのかと思って、急いでそっちを見ましたが、外はいちめんのうつくしい砂子と白いすすきの波ばかり、あの鳥捕りの広いせなかも尖った帽子も見えませんでした。

　「あの人どこへ行ったろう。」カムパネルラもぼんやりそう言っていました。

　「どこへ行ったろう。一体どこでまたあうのだろう。僕はどうしても少しあの人に物を言わなかったろう。」

　「ああ、僕もそう思っているよ。」

　「僕はあの人が邪魔なような気がしたんだ。だから僕は大へんつらい。」ジョバンニはこんな変てこな気もちは、ほんとうにはじめてだし、こんなこと今まで言ったこともないと思いました。

abrupt　「出し抜け」、突然の、急な

overhead rack　「網棚」

"Hold on, I smell apples!" said Campanella, looking around in amazement.

"Could it be because I just had apples on my mind? I smell apples too. And Seven Sisters roses!"

Giovanni looked all around, but the smell seemed to be coming from outside the window. This puzzled him all the more because it was autumn and not at all the season for Seven Sisters roses.

Before they knew it a boy about six years old, with glossy hair, wearing an unbuttoned red blazer, was standing nearby. He had a terrible expression of fear on his face, shivering and quaking in bare feet. A young man in a properly fitted black suit, as tall and straight as a zelkova tree blasted for an age by the wind, stood beside the little boy, holding him firmly by the hand.

"Oh God, where are we? Oh, it's so lovely here," said Kaoru, a little girl of about twelve with pretty brown eyes, wearing a black overcoat and clinging to the young man's arm as she stared outside in wonder.

"Why, it's Lancashire. No, it's the state of Connecticut. No, oh … we've come to the sky! We're on our way to Heaven," said the young man in black, radiating good cheer to the little girl. "See for yourself. That is the sign for Heaven. There's nothing to be afraid of now. We are being summoned by God."

But then, for some reason, deep furrows appeared on his brow and he looked weary. He tried to force a smile as he sat the little boy down next to Giovanni and gently instructed the girl to sit beside Campanella. She sat down obediently, folding her hands together on her lap.

「何だか苹果の匂がする。僕いま苹果のこと考えたためだろうか。」カムパネルラが不思議そうにあたりを見まわしました。

「ほんとうに苹果の匂だよ。それから野茨の匂もする。」ジョバンニもそこらを見ましたがやっぱりそれは窓からでも入って来るらしいのでした。いま秋だから野茨の花の匂のする筈はないとジョバンニは思いました。

そしたら俄かにそこに、つやつやした黒い髪の六つばかりの男の子が赤いジャケツのぼたんもかけずひどくびっくりしたような顔をしてがたがたふるえてはだしで立っていました。隣りには黒い洋服をきちんと着たせいの高い青年が一ぱいに風に吹かれているけやきの木のような姿勢で、男の子の手をしっかりひいて立っていました。

「あら、ここどこでしょう。まあ、きれいだわ。」青年のうしろにもひとり十二ばかりの眼の茶いろな可愛らしい女の子が黒い外套を着て青年の腕にすがって不思議そうに窓の外を見ているのでした。

「ああ、ここはランカシャイヤだ。いや、コンネクテカット州だ。いや、ああ、ぼくたちはそらへ来たのだ。わたしたちは天へ行くのです。ごらんなさい。あのしるしは天上のしるしです。もうなんにもこわいことありません。わたくしたちは神さまに召されているのです。」黒服の青年はよろこびにかがやいてその女の子に言いました。けれどもなぜかまた額に深く皺を刻んで、それに大へんつかれているらしく、無理に笑いながら男の子をジョバンニのとなりに座らせました。

それから女の子にやさしくカムパネルラのとなりの席を指さしました。女の子はすなおにそこへ座って、きちんと両手を組み合せました。

Seven Sisters roses 「野茨」。セブンシスターズローズは、野ばらの一種で別名 Rosa Multiflora Platyphylla

zelkova tree 「けやきの木」

Lancashire 「ランカシャイヤ」

summoned 「召されて」、召喚された

furrows （眉間の）「皺」

obediently 「すなおに」、従順に

The little boy had an odd expression on his face. "I'm going to see my big sister, Kikuyo," he told the young man, who had just seated himself opposite the lighthouse keeper.

The young man, unable to say a word, stared with the saddest eyes at the little boy's wavy soaking-wet hair. Suddenly the little girl put her hands to her face and sobbed.

"Your father and your sister, Kikuyo, still have lots of work to do," said the young man. "But they'll be along someday soon. More than that, just think of how long your mother has been waiting for you. She's waiting and worrying and imagining the songs that her sweet little boy, Tadashi, would be singing. She would be picturing you holding hands with the other children and skipping round and round the elderberry bushes when snow falls in the morning. So let's go right now and see mummy!"

"Okay, but I still would rather have not got on that ship in the first place."

"I know, but look up. See? That fantastic river, see it? The milky-white place in the sky that you used to see from your window all summer long and sing, *Twinkle, Twinkle, Little Star* ... it's right there! See how lovely it is, shining so brightly?"

「ぼくおおねえさんのとこへ行くんだよう。」腰掛けたばかりの男の子は顔を変にして燈台看守の向うの席に座ったばかりの青年に言いました。青年は何とも言えず悲しそうな顔をして、じっとその子の、ちぢれてぬれた頭を見ました。女の子は、いきなり両手を顔にあててしくしく泣いてしまいました。

「お父さんやきくよねえさんはまだいろいろお仕事があるのです。けれどももうすぐあとからいらっしゃいます。それよりも、おっかさんはどんなに永く待っていらっしゃったでしょう。わたしの大事なタダシはいまどんな歌をうたっているだろう、雪の降る朝にみんなと手をつないでぐるぐるにわとこのやぶをまわってあそんでいるだろうかと考えたりほんとうに待って心配していらっしゃるんですから、早く行っておっかさんにお目にかかりましょうね。」

「うん、だけど僕、船に乗らなけゃよかったなあ。」

「ええ、けれど、ごらんなさい、そら、どうです、あの立派な川、ね、あすこはあの夏中、ツウィンクル、ツウィンクル、リトル、スター　をうたってやすむとき、いつも窓からぼんやり白く見えていたでしょう。あすこですよ。ね、きれいでしょう、あんなに光っています。」

elderberry bushes
「にわとこのやぶ」

The little girl, who had been crying, wiped her eyes with a handkerchief and looked outside.

"We have nothing to be sad about anymore," explained the young man calmly to them. "We're traveling through this fine place and soon we will be in God's house, where it will be as bright as bright can be, the smells are sweet and the people are truly grand. All of the people who went in the lifeboats in our place will surely be saved and will go back to their own mothers and fathers who are so worried about them or to their own homes and children. Now, we'll be there soon, so cheer up and sing out."

The young man consoled them, stroking the little boy's wet black hair. Gradually his own expression brightened too.

"Where did you people come from?" asked the lighthouse keeper, finally beginning to catch on. "What brought you here?"

The young man gave a faraway smile.

イラスト：ルーシー・バルバース

　泣いていた姉もハンケチで眼をふいて外を見ました。青年は教えるようにそっと姉弟にまた言いました。

　「わたしたちはもうなんにもかなしいことないのです。わたしたちはこんないいとこを旅して、じき神さまのとこへ行きます。そこならもうほんとうに明るくて匂がよくて立派な人たちでいっぱいです。そしてわたしたちの代りにボートへ乗れた人たちは、きっとみんな助けられて、心配して待っているめいめいのお父さんやお母さんや自分のお家へやら行くのです。さあ、もうじきですから元気を出しておもしろくうたって行きましょう。」青年は男の子のぬれたような黒い髪をなで、みんなを慰めながら、自分もだんだん顔いろがかがやいて来ました。

　「あなた方はどちらからいらっしゃったのですか。どうなすったのですか。」さっきの燈台看守がやっと少しわかったように青年にたずねました。青年はかすかにわらいました。

consoled 「慰めながら」
lighthouse keeper 「燈台看守」

"Well, the ship hit an iceberg and sank," he said. "Their father was called home unexpectedly two months ago, so we waited and set off later. I was a university student hired as their private tutor. But then, just four days out, today, or maybe, yesterday, the ship hit an iceberg, listed just like that, then began to sink. There was some hazy moonlight that night but the fog was extremely thick. Half of the lifeboats on the port side had gone under and there weren't enough left to carry everyone.

"I realized that in a moment the whole ship would be lost, so I cried out with all my might for somebody to help save these children. The people nearby made a path for them and started to pray, but there were still many little children and their parents standing between us and the lifeboats, and I didn't have the heart to push them aside. Yet, I still felt that it was my duty to save these little ones, so I tried to elbow my way past the children in front.

"Then it dawned on me that, better than saving them in that way, I should bring them just as they are now before God. Then I thought I should save them and take on the entire sin against God by myself. But there was no way for me to do it. It tore me up inside to see mothers going crazy throwing kisses to their children in the lifeboats and fathers standing stiffly on deck holding back their tears.

「いえ、氷山にぶっつかって船が沈みましてね、わたしたちはこちらのお父さんが急な用で二ヶ月前一足さきに本国へお帰りになったのであとから発ったのです。私は大学へはいっていて、家庭教師にやとわれていたのです。ところがちょうど十二日目、今日か昨日のあたりです、船が氷山にぶっつかって一ぺんに傾きもう沈みかけました。月のあかりはどこかぼんやりありましたが、霧が非常に深かったのです。ところがボートは左舷の方半分はもうだめになっていましたから、とてもみんなは乗り切らないのです。もうそのうちにも船は沈みますし、私は必死となって、どうか小さな人たちを乗せて下さいと叫びました。近くの人たちはすぐみちを開いてそして子供たちのために祈って呉れました。けれどもそこからボートまでのところにはまだまだ小さな子どもたちや親たちやなんか居て、とても押しのける勇気がなかったのです。それでもわたくしはどうしてもこの方たちをお助けするのが私の義務だと思いましたから前にいる子供らを押しのけようとしました。けれどもまたそんなにして助けてあげるよりはこのまま神のお前にみんなで行く方がほんとうにこの方たちの幸福だとも思いました。それからまたその神にそむく罪はわたくしひとりでしょってぜひとも助けてあげようと思いました。けれどもどうして見ているとそれができないのでした。子どもらばかりボートの中へはなしてやってお母さんが狂気のようにキスを送りお父さんがかなしいのをじっとこらえてまっすぐに立っているなどとてももう腸もちぎれるようでした。

　[以降の文については、本書では改行して改ページをしているが、原作では改行なしで続いている]

have the heart to...
〜する勇気がある
elbow my way 「(肘で)押しのけようと」
tore me up 「腸もちぎれる」、ズタズタに切り裂いた

"I knew that the ship was going down fast, so, resigned to fate, I embraced these two little ones, determined to stay afloat for as long as possible. Someone threw a lifebuoy at us but it slipped and flew way out of reach. I frantically ripped some latticework from the deck and we clung on to it. Suddenly, as if from nowhere, someone was singing a hymn, and soon everyone joined in in many different languages.

"Then we heard a loud boom and we were plunged into the water. I held on tightly to these two, but we must have been caught in a whirlpool because everything vanished and the next thing we knew we found ourselves here. Their mother passed away two years ago now. Oh yes, the lifeboats must have been safely away from the ship when it sank, I mean, what else would you expect with all those seasoned sailors rowing them?"

Faint prayers could be heard, and Giovanni and Campanella, their eyes smarting, recalled things that had slipped out of their mind.

Oh, I wonder if that big ocean was the Pacific. And someone is working his life away in a far northern corner of that ocean where the icebergs float, battling the wind and the frozen tide and the violent cold in a little boat. I really feel sorry for that man, really sorry! What can I do to make him happy?

That is what Giovanni thought, his head bowed in grief.

そのうち船はもうずんずん沈みますから、私はもうすっかり覚悟してこの人たち二人を抱いて、浮べるだけは浮ぼうとかたまって船の沈むのを待っていました。誰が投げたかライフブイが一つ飛んで来ましたけれども滑ってずうっと向うへ行ってしまいました。私は一生けん命で甲板の格子になったとこをはなして、三人それにしっかりとりつきました。どこからともなく〔約二字分空白〕番の声があがりました。たちまちみんなはいろいろな国語で一ぺんにそれをうたいました。そのとき俄かに大きな音がして私たちは水に落ちもう渦に入ったと思いながらしっかりこの人たちをだいてそれからぼうっとしたと思ったらもうここへ来ていたのです。この方たちのお母さんは一昨年没くなられました。ええボートはきっと助かったにちがいありません、何せよほど熟練な水夫たちが漕いですばやく船からはなれていましたから。」

　そこらから小さないのりの声が聞えジョバンニもカムパネルラもいままで忘れていたいろいろのことをぼんやり思い出して眼が熱くなりました。

　（ああ、その大きな海はパシフィックというのではなかったろうか。その氷山の流れる北のはての海で、小さな船に乗って、風や凍りつく潮水や、烈しい寒さとたたかって、たれかが一生けんめいはたらいている。ぼくはそのひとにほんとうに気の毒でそしてすまないような気がする。ぼくはそのひとのさいわいのためにいったいどうしたらいいのだろう。）ジョバンニは首を垂れて、すっかりふさぎ込んでしまいました。

resigned to fate 「すっかり覚悟して」、運命だと思ってあきらめて

lifebuoy 「ライフブイ」、救命浮標

frantically 「一生けん命」、必死に

latticework 「格子」

clung 「とりつきました」、しがみつきました

hymn 賛美歌

＊初期稿では、〔約二字分空白〕には、讃美歌320番「主よ、みもとに近づかん」の歌詞が書かれていた

whirlpool 「渦」

frozen tide 「凍りつく潮水」

"Who knows what happiness is?" said the lighthouse keeper, comforting him. "So long as you're on the proper road, no matter how trying a thing may be, you'll be getting closer, one step at a time, up and down the high points and the low points to real happiness."

"Yes, that's true," said the young man in a reverential tone. "To attain the truest happiness you must first know all kinds of sorrow, for such is God's will."

The little brother and sister, Tadashi and Kaoru, were already sunk deep down into their seats, fast asleep. They now had soft white shoes on their feet where there had been nothing before.

The little train chugged and clanked, making its way along the phosphorescent bank of the river, with fields appearing through the windows on the other side as if in a magic lantern. Hundreds and thousands of triangular turrets of every size stretched to the very edge of the fields, the larger ones topped with red-dotted surveyors' flags so thick and dense that on the horizon they appeared like a pale bank of mist, and from there and from further afield than anyone could see, signal fires and flares of all kinds shot up one after the other into the dark violet sky. The breeze, clear and lovely, was filled with the scent of roses.

"Want one? I bet you've never had apples like these before."

The lighthouse keeper across the aisle was carefully holding large beautiful golden and red apples in his lap.

"Wow, where'd those come from?" said the young man, genuinely impressed and taken aback. "They're incredible! I didn't know they had apples like those around here." He tilted his head, fixing his squinted eyes on the bunch of apples in the man's lap.

「なにがしあわせかわからないです。ほんとうにどんなつらいことでもそれがただしいみちを進む中でのできごとなら峠の上りも下りもみんなほんとうの幸福に近づく一あしずつですから。」

燈台守がなぐさめていました。

「ああそうです。ただいちばんのさいわいに至るためにいろいろのかなしみもみんなおぼしめしです。」

青年が祈るようにそう答えました。

そしてあの姉弟はもうつかれてめいめいぐったり席によりかかって睡（ねむ）っていました。さっきのあのはだしだった足にはいつか白い柔らかな靴（くつ）をはいていたのです。

ごとごとごとごと汽車はきらびやかな燐光（りんこう）の川の岸を進みました。向うの方の窓を見ると、野原はまるで幻燈のようでした。百も千もの大小さまざまの三角標、その大きなものの上には赤い点点をうった測量旗も見え、野原のはてはそれらがいちめん、たくさんたくさん集ってぼおっと青白い霧のよう、そこからかまたはもっと向うからかときどきさまざまの形のぼんやりした狼煙（のろし）のようなものが、かわるがわるきれいな桔梗（ききょう）いろのそらにうちあげられるのでした。じつにそのすきとおった奇麗な風は、ばらの匂（におい）でいっぱいでした。

「いかがですか。こういう苹果（りんご）はおはじめてでしょう。」向うの席の燈台看守がいつか黄金（きん）と紅でうつくしくいろどられた大きな苹果を落さないように両手で膝（ひざ）の上にかかえていました。

「おや、どっから来たのですか。立派ですねえ。ここらではこんな苹果ができるのですか。」青年はほんとうにびっくりしたらしく燈台看守の両手にかかえられた一もりの苹果を眼を細くしたり首をまげたりしながらわれを忘れてながめていました。

proper road 「ただしいみち」

in a reverential tone 「祈るように」、うやうやしく

surveyors' flags 「測量旗」

further afield 「もっとむこう」、はるか遠く

squinted eyes 細目

"Well, anyway, help yourself. Come on, don't be shy."

The young man glanced at Giovanni and Campanella, taking an apple for himself.

"And you little tykes there. Come on, come an' get 'em."

Giovanni didn't much fancy being called a "little tyke," so he just sat tight in silence. But Campanella thanked the lighthouse keeper. At this the young man took two apples and handed them to the boys. Giovanni rose to his feet and thanked the man too.

The lighthouse keeper, who could now manage to carry the rest of the apples by himself, went to the little brother and sister and gently placed one apple each in their lap.

"Thank you very much," said the young man looking on. "Where do they grow apples as lovely as these?"

"Of course this region is farmland, but generally speaking things just grow by themselves. Farming shouldn't break anybody's back. All you do here is sow the seed of your choice and, day by day, the plant grows of its own accord. And the rice here isn't like your rice around the Pacific Ocean, because it's got no husks, and besides, the grains are ten times bigger and they smell absolutely delicious.

"They don't farm up where you're headin', though, but you can eat the apples and cakes there down to the very last morsel, and you'll find yourself giving off a faint sweet aroma through your own pores, a different aroma for each person!"

Suddenly Tadashi blinked his eyes open.

「いや、まあおとり下さい。どうか、まあおとり下さい。」

青年は一つとってジョバンニたちの方をちょっと見ました。

「さあ、向うの坊ちゃんがた。いかがですか。おとり下さい。」

ジョバンニは坊ちゃんといわれたのですこししゃくにさわってだまっていましたがカムパネルラは

「ありがとう、」と言いました。すると青年は自分でとって一つずつ二人に送ってよこしましたのでジョバンニも立ってありがとうと言いました。

燈台看守はやっと両腕があいたのでこんどは自分で一つずつ睡（ねむ）っている姉弟の膝にそっと置きました。

「どうもありがとう。どこでできるのですか。こんな立派な苹果（りんご）は。」

青年はつくづく見ながら言いました。

「この辺ではもちろん農業はいたしますけれども大ていひとりでにいいものができるような約束になって居ります。農業だってそんなに骨は折れはしません。たいてい自分の望む種子（たね）さえ播（ま）けばひとりでにどんどんできます。米だってパシフィック辺のように殻もないし十倍も大きくて匂もいいのです。けれどもあなたがたのいらっしゃる方なら農業はもうありません。苹果だってお菓子だってかすが少しもありませんからみんなそのひとそのひとによってちがったわずかのいいかおりになって毛あなからちらけてしまうのです。」

にわかに男の子がぱっちり眼をあいて言いました。

"Oh, I was just dreaming of my mother," he said. "She was standing by this great big cupboard or bookshelf or something and she was holding out her hand and looking at me and smiling so big. I said, 'Mummy, do you want me to get an apple for you?' And that's when I just woke up. Gee, this is the same train I was on before."

"You've got an apple," said the young man. "This nice man gave us all one."

"Thank you, sir. Hey, Kaoru's still asleep. I'll wake her up, okay? Sis? Look, we got apples. Wake up and see!"

Kaoru smiled and opened her eyes, rubbing them with both hands from the glare. Then she saw the apples. Tadashi was munching away at an apple as if it was a piece of pie. The peel that he had taken the trouble to peel off took on the shape of a corkscrew as it fell, turned smoky gray, flared and evaporated before reaching the floor.

Giovanni and Campanella stashed their apples in their pockets for safe keeping.

Downstream there was a vast forest growing on the far bank of the river, its thick and deep blue branches loaded down with round ripe fruit, glowing red, a staggeringly tall triangular turret standing in its very center. The breeze from the forest carried the indescribably beautiful sound of bells and xylophones that mingled with everything, permeating the air.

The young man shuddered, spellbound by the sound.

They all listened to the music in silence as the sky unfolded into what looked like a yellow and light-green meadow or carpet, and pure white dewdrops, like wax, swept across the face of a sun.

"Oh, look at those crows!" cried Kaoru, who was now beside Campanella.

「ああぼくいまお母さんの夢をみていたよ。お母さんがね立派な戸棚や本のあるとこに居てね、ぼくの方を見て手をだしてにこにこにこにこわらったよ。ぼくおっかさん。りんごをひろってきてあげましょうか言ったら眼がさめちゃった。ああここさっきの汽車のなかだねえ。」

「その苹果がそこにあります。このおじさんにいただいたのですよ。」青年が言いました。

「ありがとうおじさん。おや、かおるねえさんまだねてるねえ、ぼくおこしてやろう。ねえさん。ごらん、りんごをもらったよ。おきてごらん。」

姉はわらって眼をさましまぶしそうに両手を眼にあててそれから苹果を見ました。男の子はまるでパイを喰べ（た）るようにもうそれを喰べていました、また折角剥いたそのきれいな皮も、くるくるコルク抜きのような形になって床へ落ちるまでの間にはすうっと、灰いろに光って蒸発してしまうのでした。

二人はりんごを大切にポケットにしまいました。

川下の向う岸に青く茂った大きな林が見え、その枝には熟してまっ赤に光る円い実がいっぱい、その林のまん中に高い高い三角標が立って、森の中からはオーケストラベルやジロフォンにまじって何とも言えずきれいな音いろが、とけるように浸（し）みるように風につれて流れて来るのでした。

青年はぞくっとしてからだをふるうようにしました。

だまってその譜を聞いていると、そこらにいちめん黄いろやうすい緑の明るい野原か敷物かがひろがり、またまっ白な蝋（ろう）のような露が太陽の面を擦（かす）めて行くように思われました。

「まあ、あの烏（からす）。」カムパネルラのとなりのかおると呼ばれた女の子が叫びました。

corkscrew 「コルク抜き」

stashed 「しまいました」、隠した

loaded down with... 「〜がいっぱい」、〜を抱えて

staggeringly びっくりするほど

permeating the air 空気に広がって（充満して、満ちて）

shuddered 身震いした

spellbound 魔法にかかって、うっとりと

meadow 「野原」、牧草地

銀河鉄道の夜　103

"Those aren't crows, they're magpies," exclaimed Campanella in what came out as a scolding voice, causing Giovanni to laugh unintentionally and the little girl to feel suddenly awkward.

Black birds in their thousands had come to rest in rows along the milky-white bank, bathing motionlessly in the glow coming off the river.

"Yes, they are magpies," interceded the young man. "You can tell by the tuft sticking out of their head."

By now the tall turret in the blue forest was face to face with the train, and the familiar strains of a hymn's melody could be heard coming from the wagons in the very back. It sounded like it was being sung by a huge chorus of people. The young man turned pale and wan, started to rise and follow the sound, but decided to sit down again.

Kaoru buried her face in her handkerchief and even Giovanni couldn't help but get a bit sniffly. Somehow the melody was picked up by someone, until both Giovanni and Campanella found themselves singing along in unison.

The blue torchwood grove sparkling on the invisible far bank of the celestial river moved gradually back and beyond, while the music from the mysterious instruments streaming out of it was almost completely drowned out by the chugging of the train and the rush of the wind.

"Look, a peacock!" cried Tadashi.

"Peacocks, lots of them," said Kaoru.

Giovanni was watching the reflection of light flickering off the peacocks as they spread and closed their pale feathers above the grove now no bigger than a miniature green shell button.

"Right," said Campanella to Kaoru. "It was peacock calls we heard before."

「からすでない。みんなかささぎだ。」カムパネルラが
また何気なく叱るように叫びましたので、ジョバンニは
また思わず笑い、女の子はきまり悪そうにしました。まっ
たく河原の青じろいあかりの上に、黒い鳥がたくさんた
くさんいっぱいに列になってとまってじっと川の微光を
受けているのでした。

「かささぎですねえ、頭のうしろのとこに毛がぴんと延
びてますから。」青年はとりなすように言いました。

　向うの青い森の中の三角標はすっかり汽車の正面に来
ました。そのとき汽車のずうっとうしろの方からあの聞き
なれた〔約二字分空白〕番の讃美歌のふしが聞えてきまし
た。よほどの人数で合唱しているらしいのでした。青年は
さっと顔いろが青ざめ、たって一ぺんそっちへ行きそうに
しましたが思いかえしてまた座りました。かおる子はハン
ケチを顔にあててしまいました。ジョバンニまで何だか鼻
が変になりました。けれどもいつともなく誰ともなくその
歌は歌い出されだんだんはっきり強くなりました。思わず
ジョバンニもカムパネルラも一緒にうたい出したのです。

　そして青い橄欖の森が見えない天の川の向うにさめざ
めと光りながらだんだんうしろの方へ行ってしまいそこ
から流れて来るあやしい楽器の音ももう汽車のひびきや
風の音にすり耗らされてずうっとかすかになりました。

「あ孔雀が居るよ。」

「ええたくさん居たわ。」女の子がこたえました。

　ジョバンニはその小さく小さくなっていまはもう一つ
の緑いろの貝ぼたんのように見える森の上にさっさっと
青じろく時々光ってその孔雀がはねをひろげたりとじた
りする光の反射を見ました。

「そうだ、孔雀の声だってさっき聞えた。」カムパネル
ラがかおる子に言いました。

magpies 「かささぎ」

interceded 介入した

strains of a hymn's
melody 「讃美歌のふ
し」、讃美歌の旋律

wan 「青ざめ」、血の気
のない

sniffly 「鼻が変になり」、
鼻をすすりがちな

blue torchwood
grove 「青い橄欖の森」

drowned out かき消
された

"Yes, I know," she said. "I saw about thirty of them. It was the peacocks that sounded like a harp."

Giovanni, glum yet not knowing why, wanted to glare at Campanella and say, "Hey, let's hop off here and have some fun!"

The river divided in two. A turret as high as the sky had been erected on the island at its fork, and on top of it perched a man in a red cap and loosely fitting clothes. He was looking toward the sky and signaling with red and blue flags in his hands.

He waved the red flag repeatedly in the air then suddenly brought it down, hid it behind his back and lifted the blue one as high as he could, waving it furiously, like an orchestra conductor. At that very moment an unbelievable clamor filled the air as if it had suddenly started raining cats and dogs, and whole clusters of little black birds shot, as if out of the mouth of a shotgun, across the sky to the far side of the river. Giovanni found himself sticking half his body out the window to get a good look at the tens of thousands of little birds as they flew, each and every one calling through the magnificent dark violet sky.

"Just look at those birds fly," he said from outside the window.

"Birds?" said Campanella, looking up.

The man in the loose outfit on top of the turret suddenly raised his red flag and waved it madly. At that moment the great cloud of birds froze, an earsplitting crash was heard downstream, and then it turned perfectly quiet. Yet no sooner was there quiet than did the red-capped signaler once again wave his blue flag.

「ええ、三十疋ぐらいはたしかに居たわ。ハープのように聞えたのはみんな孔雀よ。」女の子が答えました。ジョバンニは俄かに何とも言えずかなしい気がして思わず

「カムパネルラ、ここからはねおりて遊んで行こうよ。」とこわい顔をして言おうとしたくらいでした。

川は二つにわかれました。そのまっくらな島のまん中に高い高いやぐらが一つ組まれてその上に一人の寛い服を着て赤い帽子をかぶった男が立っていました。そして両手に赤と青の旗をもってそらを見上げて信号しているのでした。

ジョバンニが見ている間その人はしきりに赤い旗をふっていましたが俄かに赤旗をおろしてうしろにかくすようにし青い旗を高く高くあげてまるでオーケストラの指揮者のように烈しく振りました。すると空中にざあっと雨のような音がして何かまっくらなものがいくかたまりもいくかたまりも鉄砲丸のように川の向うの方へ飛んで行くのでした。ジョバンニは思わず窓からからだを半分出してそっちを見あげました。美しい美しい桔梗いろのがらんとした空の下を実に何万という小さな鳥どもが幾組も幾組もめいめいせわしくせわしく鳴いて通って行くのでした。

「鳥が飛んで行くな。」ジョバンニが窓の外で言いました。

「どら、」カムパネルラもそらを見ました。そのときあのやぐらの上のゆるい服の男は俄かに赤い旗をあげて狂気のようにふりうごかしました。するとぴたっと鳥の群は通らなくなりそれと同時にぴしゃんという潰れたような音が川下の方で起ってそれからしばらくしいんとしました。と思ったらあの赤帽の信号手がまた青い旗をふって叫んでいたのです。

glum　浮かない顔の、不機嫌な、むっつりした
turret　「やぐら」
clamor　騒音、喧騒
earsplitting　「ぴしゃぁんという」、つんざくような

"Now is the time for all migratory birds to migrate! Now is the time for all migratory birds to migrate!" he yelled in a voice as clear as a bell.

And once again the great mass of countless birds shot overhead. Kaoru poked her head out of the same middle window as the two boys, facing upwards with lovely sparkling cheeks.

"Oh, so many birds!" she said to Giovanni. "And the sky is so pretty too!"

But Giovanni turned a deaf ear to Kaoru, keeping his mouth shut, considering her no more than a big pain in the neck and continuing to look up at the sky.

Kaoru took a faint breath, fell silent and returned to her seat. Campanella, feeling sorry for her, drew his head back inside and concentrated on his map.

"Is that man there to guide the birds?" she asked Campanella faintly.

"He's there giving signals to migrating birds," he replied, unsure of himself. "I mean, a flare rockets up or something, telling him to do it."

Silence filled the wagon. Giovanni wanted to bring his head in from the window, but the bright light inside would be too hard to bear, so he remained as he was and whistled a tune.

Why am I so forlorn? I should be a kinder person, a more generous person. I can see a small blue flame, hazy with smoke, way beyond the far bank. It is so quiet and cold, but it calms my spirit if I keep my mind on it.

「いまこそわたれわたり鳥、いまこそわたれわたり鳥。」その声もはっきり聞えました。それといっしょにまた幾万という鳥の群がそらをまっすぐにかけたのです。二人の顔を出しているまん中の窓からあの女の子が顔を出して美しい頬をかがやかせながらそらを仰ぎました。

「まあ、この鳥、たくさんですわねえ、あらまあそらのきれいなこと。」女の子はジョバンニにはなしかけましたけれどもジョバンニは生意気ないやだいと思いながらだまって口をむすんでそらを見あげていました。

女の子は小さくほっと息をしてだまって席へ戻りました。カムパネルラが気の毒そうに窓から顔を引っ込めて地図を見ていました。

「あの人鳥へ教えてるんでしょうか。」女の子がそっとカムパネルラにたずねました。

「わたり鳥へ信号してるんです。きっとどこからかのろしがあがるためでしょう。」カムパネルラが少しおぼつかなそうに答えました。そして車の中はしぃんとなりました。ジョバンニはもう頭を引っ込めたかったのですけれども明るいとこへ顔を出すのがつらかったのでだまってこらえてそのまま立って口笛を吹いていました。

（どうして僕はこんなにかなしいのだろう。僕はもっとこころもちをきれいに大きくもたなければいけない。あすこの岸のずうっと向うにまるでけむりのような小さな青い火が見える。あれはほんとうにしずかでつめたい。僕はあれをよく見てこころもちをしずめるんだ。）

［以降の文については、本書では改行して改ページをしているが、原作では改行なしで続いている］

a big pain in the neck　面倒、厄介

a flare rockets up「のろしがあがる」

forlorn　「かなしい」、わびしい、心細い

Giovanni, gazing in the distance, grasped his burning, throbbing head in both hands.

Is there really nobody who will stick with me to the edges of the universe and beyond? Campanella just sits there jabbering away to that little girl, and it hurts me more than anybody knows.

Giovanni's eyes filled with tears, making the Milky Way seem even more remote and dreamy white.

By this time the train had veered away from the river, passing above a cliff. The black cliff face on the opposite bank loomed gradually higher and higher at the lower reaches of the river. A huge stand of corn flashed into view, with leaves that were all frizzled and curly and husks that were big and already a striking green, sprouting red hairs and brimming with kernels like pearls.

Soon the number of plants had multiplied until the stand, with plants in rows, lined the area between the cliff and the track.

When Giovanni pulled his head in and looked through the windows across the aisle he saw ears of corn swaying in the breeze, growing all the way to the horizon, laden with red and green dewdrops on the tips of their curly leaves, shining like diamonds that had absorbed the rays of the sun.

"That's corn, isn't it?" said Campanella to Giovanni.

But Giovanni wasn't in a mood to be cheered up and sat there gazing at the field with a moony face.

"Guess so," he answered.

That's when the train slowed down, passed by a few signals and illuminated switches and came to a halt at a little station.

ジョバンニは熱って痛いあたまを両手で押えるようにしてそっちの方を見ました。（ああほんとうにどこまでもどこまでも僕といっしょに行くひとはないだろうか。カムパネルラだってあんな女の子とおもしろそうに談しているし僕はほんとうにつらいなあ。）ジョバンニの眼はまた泪でいっぱいになり天の川もまるで遠くへ行ったようにぼんやり白く見えるだけでした。

　そのとき汽車はだんだん川からはなれて崖の上を通るようになりました。向う岸もまた黒いいろの崖が川の岸を下流に下るにしたがってだんだん高くなって行くのでした。そしてちらっと大きなとうもろこしの木を見ました。その葉はぐるぐるに縮れ葉の下にはもう美しい緑いろの大きな苞が赤い毛を吐いて真珠のような実もちらっと見えたのでした。それはだんだん数を増して来てもういまは列のように崖と線路との間にならび思わずジョバンニが窓から顔を引っ込めて向う側の窓を見ましたときは美しいそらの野原の地平線のはてまでその大きなとうもろこしの木がほとんどいちめんに植えられてさやさや風にゆらぎその立派なちぢれた葉のさきからはまるでひるの間にいっぱい日光を吸った金剛石のように露がいっぱいについて赤や緑やきらきら燃えて光っているのでした。カムパネルラが「あれとうもろこしだねえ」とジョバンニに言いましたけれどもジョバンニはどうしても気持がなおりませんでしたからただぶっきり棒に野原を見たまま「そうだろう。」と答えました。そのとき汽車はだんだんしずかになっていくつかのシグナルとてんてつ器の灯を過ぎ小さな停車場にとまりました。

throbbing　ズキズキする

jabbering away　ぺちゃくちゃしゃべり続ける

veered away　「はなれて」、（方向が）逸れて

loomed　ぼんやりと現れた、そびえ立った

frizzled　縮らせた

kernels　「実」、種子や殻粒などの食べれる部分

laden with...　「いっぱい〜について」

moony face　気の抜けた顔、気乗りしない顔

switches　「てんてつ器」

The pale-white clock face opposite them indicated precisely the Second Hour, the wind died down, the train was still, and a pendulum ticktocked the time throughout the still field. Then a faint melody, perfectly in time with the regular ticking of the clock, wafted their way, a thread of sound from the farthest fringe of the field.

"It's the New World Symphony," said Kaoru to herself.

All the people in the train, including the stately young man in black, were plunged into a tender dream.

Why can't I cheer myself up in such a peaceful place as this? Why am I so alone? And that Campanella, he's really being mean. We're on this train together and all he does is blabber to that girl. It's really hard to take!

Giovanni, his face half buried in his palms, stared out the window on the other side. A flutelike note, clear as glass, rang out and the train began to creep along, as Campanella sadly whistled the tune of "Once Around the Stars."

"Precisely, precisely, you see, it's all towering plateaus up here," blurted out an old man from behind, as if he had just woken up. "Now, if it's corn you want, you gotta open up a hole two feet deep and plant the seed in that, otherwise you haven't got a prayer."

"Is that right? I guess we won't be reaching the river for quite some time yet."

"Precisely, precisely. We're still a good two thousand to six thousand feet above her. We're over one hell of a gorge here."

その正面の青じろい時計はかっきり第二時を示しその振子は風もなくなり汽車もうごかずしずかなしずかな野原のなかにカチッカチッと正しく時を刻んで行くのでした。

　そしてまったくその振子の音のたえまを遠くの遠くの野原のはてから、かすかなかすかな旋律が糸のように流れて来るのでした。「新世界交響楽だわ。」姉がひとりごとのようにこっちを見ながらそっと言いました。全くもう車の中ではあの黒服の丈高い青年も誰もみんなやさしい夢を見ているのでした。

　（こんなしずかないいとこで僕はどうしてもっと愉快になれないだろう。どうしてこんなにひとりさびしいのだろう。けれどもカムパネルラなんかあんまりひどい、僕といっしょに汽車に乗っていながらまるであんな女の子とばかり談しているんだもの。僕はほんとうにつらい。）ジョバンニはまた両手で顔を半分かくすようにして向うの窓のそとを見つめていました。すきとおった硝子のような笛が鳴って汽車はしずかに動き出し、カムパネルラもさびしそうに星めぐりの口笛を吹きました。

　「ええ、ええ、もうこの辺はひどい高原ですから。」うしろの方で誰かとしよりらしい人のいま眼がさめたという風ではきはき談している声がしました。

　「とうもろこしだって棒で二尺も孔をあけておいてそこへ播かないと生えないんです。」

　「そうですか。川まではよほどありましょうかねえ、」

　「えええええ河までは二千尺から六千尺あります。もうまるでひどい峡谷になっているんです。」

pendulum 「振子」
wafted their way 「流れてくる」
New World Symphony 「新世界交響楽」
blabber おしゃべりする
plateaus 「高原」
gorge 「峡谷」

It dawned on Giovanni ...

Sure, we're over the Colorado Plateau!

Kaoru, far away in thought, her face like an apple wrapped in silk, was staring in the same direction as Giovanni, while Campanella was still whistling sadly to himself. All of a sudden the corn was gone, leaving a vast black stretch of plain from one horizon to the other.

The New World Symphony was coming in loud and clear from beyond the horizon when an American Indian, an arrow fixed in his little bow, decked out in a white feather headdress and a variety of stones on his arms and breast, started running after the train as fast as his moccasins would take him.

"Gosh, an Indian!" cried Kaoru. "Look, it's an Indian!"

This woke up the young man in black and sent both Giovanni and Campanella to their feet.

"He's running after us!" she said. "He's running this way, chasing us!"

"No, he isn't chasing the train," said the young man, standing up and putting his hands in his pockets and forgetting where he was for the moment. "He's hunting or doing a dance."

そうそうここはコロラドの高原じゃなかったろうか、ジョバンニは思わずそう思いました。カムパネルラはまださびしそうにひとり口笛を吹き、女の子はまるで絹で包んだ苹果（りんご）のような顔いろをしてジョバンニの見る方を見ているのでした。突然とうもろこしがなくなって巨（おお）きな黒い野原がいっぱいにひらけました。新世界交響楽はいよいよはっきり地平線のはてから湧（わ）きそのまっ黒な野原のなかを一人のインデアンが白い鳥の羽根を頭につけたくさんの石を腕と胸にかざり小さな弓に矢を番（つが）えて一目散に汽車を追って来るのでした。

　「あら、インデアンですよ。インデアンですよ。ごらんなさい。」

　黒服の青年も眼をさましました。ジョバンニもカムパネルラも立ちあがりました。

　「走って来るわ、あら、走って来るわ。追いかけているんでしょう。」

　「いいえ、汽車を追ってるんじゃないんですよ。猟をするか踊るかしてるんですよ。」青年はいまどこに居るか忘れたという風にポケットに手を入れて立ちながら言いました。

dawned on...　〜にわかりはじめた

Colorado Plateau
「コロラド高原」。アメリカ合衆国西部ロッキー山脈とワサッチ山脈との間に広がる大高原

decked out　着飾った、おめかしをした

moccasins　モカシン。アメリカの先住民が履いていた革製の靴

What he was doing did look very much like a dance. His step was too measured and methodical for a dash. Then, without warning, he stopped dead in his tracks, his white headdress tumbled down in front of him and he fired his arrow quick as a flash into the air. A crane whirled dizzily down and once again he sprinted ahead to catch it in his open arms. He stopped there, beaming.

But his figure standing there holding the crane in his arms and looking in the direction of the train grew steadily smaller and ever distant, two ceramic insulators on a telegraph pole glittered by, and once again they were passing through thickets of corn. The train was moving along the top of a gigantic cliff, the wide river flowing, shining far down below it.

"Precisely," said the old man. "From here on it's all downhill. Which is not to say that it's a breeze gettin' down to river level in one go. This train can never go the other way, 'cause the angle here is too much for her. See, we're pickin' up speed already."

The train chugged faster and faster down the slope and, as it skirted the very edge of the cliff, the river shone brightly in their eyes. Giovanni's mood brightened too. They sped past a small hut with a solitary little boy standing in front of it. He cried out into the air.

まったくインデアンは半分は踊っているようでした。第一かけるにしても足のふみようがもっと経済もとれ本気にもなれそうでした。にわかにくっきり白いその羽根は前の方へ倒れるようになりインデアンはぴたっと立ちどまってすばやく弓を空にひきました。そこから一羽の鶴（つる）がふらふらと落ちて来てまた走り出したインデアンの大きくひろげた両手に落ちこみました。インデアンはうれしそうに立ってわらいました。そしてその鶴をもってこっちを見ている影ももうどんどん小さく遠くなり電しんばしらの碍子（がいし）がきらっきらっと続いて二つばかり光ってまたとうもろこしの林になってしまいました。こっち側の窓を見ますと汽車はほんとうに高い高い崖（がけ）の上を走っていてその谷の底には川がやっぱり幅ひろく明るく流れていたのです。

「ええ、もうこの辺から下りです。何せこんどは一ぺんにあの水面までおりて行くんですから容易じゃありません。この傾斜があるもんですから汽車は決して向うからこっちへは来ないんです。そらもうだんだん早くなったでしょう。」さっきの老人らしい声が言いました。

どんどんどんどん汽車は降りて行きました。崖のはじに鉄道がかかるときは川が明るく下にのぞけたのです。ジョバンニはだんだんこころもちが明るくなって来ました。汽車が小さな小屋の前を通ってその前にしょんぼりひとりの子供が立ってこっちを見ているときなどは思わずほうと叫びました。

measured　慎重な、のんびりとした

methodical　几帳面な

tumbled down　「倒れるようになり」、垂れた

sprinted　「走り出した」

beaming　「わらいました」。beam には「ニコニコ笑う、微笑む」の意味がある

it's a breeze　「容易」、簡単

solitary　ひとりぼっちの、孤独な

The train was clanking steeply down the incline even faster now, all the people in it pushed back hard against their seats, holding on for dear life. Giovanni and Campanella smiled at each other. The Milky Way was streaming furiously past them, virtually under their nose, giving off brilliant flashes of light. Large wild pinks were in bloom in spots along the pale red bank. The train slowed down by degrees, running steadily and smoothly again. Banners decorated with stars and picks were flying on either bank of the river.

"I wonder what banners those are," said Giovanni, finally managing to eke out some words.

"Beats me. Nothing like them on my map. There's an iron boat there too."

"Yeah."

"Perhaps they're building a bridge," said Kaoru.

"Sure, they're Army Engineers' banners! They're on bridge-building maneuvers. Except, I don't see any soldiers around."

Just then, a little downstream by the opposite bank, the invisible river flashed, and a pillar of water shot up high into the air with an ear-splitting boom.

"They're blasting! They're blasting!" cried Campanella, jumping for joy.

The water in the pillar disappeared, but huge salmon and trout that had been flung into the sky by the explosion remained in the air, their bellies gleaming white as they described a perfect arc before falling back into the river.

Giovanni was in such high spirits now that he wanted to leap into the air himself.

"It's the Army Engineers of the Sky!" he cried. "Fantastic! Those trout or whatever just went rocketing up like this. I've never been on such a great trip as this. Out of this world!"

どんどんどんどん汽車は走って行きました。室中のひ<ruby>へやじゅう<rt></rt></ruby>とたちは半分うしろの方へ倒れるようになりながら腰掛にしっかりしがみついていました。ジョバンニは思わずカムパネルラとわらいました。もうそして天の川は汽車のすぐ横手をいままでよほど激しく流れて来たらしくときどきちらちら光ってながれているのでした。うすあかい河原なでしこの花があちこち咲いていました。汽車はようやく落ち着いたようにゆっくりと走っていました。

　向うとこっちの岸に星のかたちとつるはしを書いた旗がたっていました。

　「あれ何の旗だろうね。」ジョバンニがやっとものを言いました。

　「さあ、わからないねえ、地図にもないんだもの。鉄の舟がおいてあるねえ。」

　「ああ。」

　「橋を架けるとこじゃないんでしょうか。」女の子が言いました。

　「あああれ工兵の旗だねえ。架橋演習をしてるんだ。けれど兵隊のかたちが見えないねえ。」

　その時向う岸ちかくの少し下流の方で見えない天の川の水がぎらっと光って柱のように高くはねあがりどぉと烈しい音がしました。<ruby>はげ<rt></rt></ruby>

　「発破だよ、発破だよ。」カムパネルラはこおどりしました。<ruby>はっぱ<rt></rt></ruby>

　その柱のようになった水は見えなくなり大きな鮭や鱒<ruby>ます<rt></rt></ruby>がきらっきらっと白く腹を光らせて空中に抛り出されて<ruby>ほう<rt></rt></ruby>円い輪を描いてまた水に落ちました。ジョバンニはもうはねあがりたいくらい気持が軽くなって言いました。

　「空の工兵大隊だ。どうだ、鱒やなんかがまるでこんな<ruby>ます<rt></rt></ruby>になってはねあげられたねえ。僕こんな愉快な旅はしたことない。いいねえ。」

clanking　ガタガタと音を立てる

for dear life　必死に

banners　「旗」

picks　「つるはし」

eke out...　何とか〜する、辛うじて〜する

Beats me.　「わからないねえ」

maneuvers　（軍事）「演習」

blasting　「発破」、爆破

trout　「鱒」

"Those trout would be this big close up," said Campanella. "This river is just crawling with fish."

"I wonder if there are little fish too," said Kaoru, now hooked on the boys' conversation.

"There's bound to be," replied Giovanni, smiling at her and feeling his old self again. "If they've got big ones, they'd be bound to have little ones too. We're just too far away to see them."

"Look, those must be the palaces where the twins live," exclaimed Tadashi, suddenly pointing out the window.

Two little shrines that might have been fashioned of crystal stood roof to roof on top of a rolling hill to their right.

"What's the palaces where the twins live?"

"Our mother told us about them lots of times," explained Kaoru. "There are two little crystal palaces next to each other just as she said there would be."

"Tell us about them. What are twin stars doing in the sky?"

"Why don't you ask me?" said Tadashi. "The twins went to the fields to play. Then they had an argument with a crow, see?"

"No, that's not how it went," said Kaoru. "Let's see now. It was on the bank of the Milky Way, mummy said so, she ..."

"And the comet came whooshing by. Whoosh! Whoosh!"

"Stop it, Tadashi! That's not the way it was. That's a different story altogether."

"So it's them playing that flute?" asked Giovanni.

"They're off at sea," said Tadashi.

"No they're not!" insisted Kaoru. "They've already been to sea."

"Yeah I know, I know," continued Tadashi. "I can tell you all about it."

「あの鱒なら近くで見たらこれくらいあるねえ、たくさんさかな居るんだな、この水の中に。」

「小さなお魚もいるんでしょうか。」女の子が談《はなし》につり込まれて言いました。

「居るんでしょう。大きなのが居るんだから小さいのもいるんでしょう。けれど遠くだからいま小さいの見えなかったねえ。」ジョバンニはもうすっかり機嫌《きげん》が直って面白そうにわらって女の子に答えました。

「あれきっと双子のお星さまのお宮だよ。」男の子がいきなり窓の外をさして叫びました。

右手の低い丘の上に小さな水晶ででもこさえたような二つのお宮がならんで立っていました。

「双子のお星さまのお宮って何だい。」

「あたし前になんべんもお母さんから聴いたわ。ちゃんと小さな水晶のお宮で二つならんでいるからきっとそうだわ。」

「はなしてごらん。双子のお星さまが何したっての。」

「ぼくも知ってらい。双子のお星さまが野原へ遊びにでてからすと喧嘩《けんか》したんだろう。」

「そうじゃないわよ。あのね、天の川の岸にね、おっかさんお話なすったわ、……」

「それから彗星《ほうきぼし》がギーギーフーギーギーフーて言って来たねえ。」

「いやだわたあちゃんそうじゃないわよ。それはべつの方だわ。」

「するとあすこにいま笛を吹いて居るんだろうか。」

「いま海へ行ってらあ。」

「いけないわよ。もう海からあがっていらっしゃったのよ。」

「そうそう。ぼく知ってらあ、ぼくおはなししよう。」

hooked on... 「〜につり込まれて」、〜に引っかかって

feeling his old self 「すっかり機嫌が直って」

comet 「彗星」

whooshing 「ギーギーフー」、シューという音を立てる

The opposite bank of the invisible river turned red all of a sudden and its waves glittered like needles, throwing willows and everything into stark silhouette. A large crimson fire was blazing in a distant field, its towering smoke threatening to char the deep violet of the sky. The dancing flame was more transparent red than a ruby, more exquisite than lithium.

"I wonder what's causing that fire," said Giovanni. "What could be burning to give off a flame as red as that?"

"It's Scorpio's fire," replied Campanella, his head buried in his map.

"Oh I know about Scorpio's fire," said Kaoru.

"So what is it then?" asked Giovanni.

"Scorpio burnt to death. My father told me millions of times that the fire burns to this very day."

"A scorpion's an insect, right?"

"Uh-huh, it is. But it's a nice insect," said Kaoru.

"A scorpion's not a nice insect! I saw one in alcohol at the museum. It's got a huge stinger on his tail, and the teacher said if it stings you, you die!"

"I know, but it's still a nice insect. My father told me that a long long time ago Scorpio lived in a field in Baldola, and he survived by killing teeny bugs and eating them up. Then one day he was caught by a weasel and it looked like he was going to be eaten up himself. He tried to get away with all his might and he was about to be pinned down by the weasel when out of the blue there was this well in front of him and he fell right down into it, and there was no way in the world he could get back up, so it looked like he was going to drown for sure. So then he began to pray ...

川の向う岸が俄かに赤くなりました。楊の木や何か
もまっ黒にすかし出され見えない天の川の波もときどき
ちらちら針のように赤く光りました。まったく向う岸の
野原に大きなまっ赤な火が燃されその黒いけむりは高く
桔梗いろのつめたそうな天をも焦がしそうでした。ルビー
よりも赤くすきとおりリチウムよりもうつくしく酔った
ようになってその火は燃えているのでした。

「あれは何の火だろう。あんな赤く光る火は何を燃やせ
ばできるんだろう。」ジョバンニが言いました。

「蝎の火だな。」カムパネルラがまた地図と首っ引きし
て答えました。

「あら、蝎の火のことならあたし知ってるわ。」

「蝎の火ってなんだい。」ジョバンニがききました。

「蝎がやけて死んだのよ。その火がいまでも燃えてるっ
てあたし何べんもお父さんから聴いたわ。」

「蝎って、虫だろう。」

「ええ、蝎は虫よ。だけどいい虫だわ。」

「蝎いい虫じゃないよ。僕博物館でアルコールにつけて
あるの見た。尾にこんなかぎがあってそれで螫されると
死ぬって先生が言ったよ。」

「そうよ。だけどいい虫だわ、お父さんこう言ったのよ。
むかしのバルドラの野原に一ぴきの蝎がいて小さな虫
やなんか殺してたべて生きていたんですって。するとあ
る日いたちに見附かって食べられそうになったんですっ
て。さそりは一生けん命遁げて遁げたけどとうといた
ちに押えられそうになったわ、そのときいきなり前に井
戸があってその中に落ちてしまったわ、もうどうしても
あがられないでさそりは溺れはじめたのよ。そのときさ
そりはこう言ってお祈りしたというの、

throwing... into stark silhouette 「真っ黒にす
かし出され」、真っ暗な影
を投じて

willows 「楊」

crimson fire 「真っ赤
な火」

char 焦げたもの、炭化
したもの

lithium 「リチウム」

Scorpio's fire 「蝎の
火」

to this very day 「今
でも」、今日のこの日まで

Baldola 「バルドラ」

teeny 「小さな」、ちっぽ
けな

weasel 「いたち」

'Oh, I can't remember how many living creatures I have killed in my lifetime, but now I found myself trapped by the weasel and running for my own life. Oh, woe is me! Everything is so risky in life. Why didn't I just give my body to the weasel and be done with it? If I had, at least he would have been able to live another day.

'Dear God, please look into my heart and in the next life don't throw away my life in vain like this, but use my body for the good and happiness of all!'

"That's what he said. And Scorpio saw his body turn bright red and ignite into a beautiful flame, lighting up the darkness of the night sky! And he's burning now too, that's what my father said. That fire ... it must be him."

"Sure, look! The triangular turrets are lined up exactly in the shape of a scorpion."

Giovanni could clearly see beyond the tower of fire. Three turrets made up a scorpion's front legs, with five others forming the tail with a hook in its stinger. The red flame burned brightly without so much as a crackle.

As the fire receded gradually into the distance, everyone began to hear all sorts of indescribably lively music, to smell what smelled like bouquets of flowers and to hear a mixed murmur of voices and whistling. There appeared to be a town nearby with some sort of festival in progress.

"Oh Centaurus, Let the Dew Fall!" cried Tadashi, who had been fast asleep until then in the seat beside Giovanni.

ああ、わたしはいままでいくつのものの命をとったか
わからない、そしてその私がこんどいたちにとられよう
としたときはあんなに一生けん命にげた。それでもとう
とうこんなになってしまった。ああなんにもあてにならな
い。どうしてわたしはわたしのからだをだまっていた
ちに呉れてやらなかったろう。そしたらいたちも一日生
きのびたろうに。どうか神さま。私の心をごらん下さい。
こんなにむなしく命をすてずどうかこの次にはまことの
みんなの幸のために私のからだをおつかい下さい。って
言ったというの。そしたらいつか蝎はじぶんのからだが
まっ赤なうつくしい火になって燃えてよるのやみを照ら
しているのを見たって。いまでも燃えてるってお父さん
仰<ruby>仰<rt>おっしゃ</rt></ruby>ったわ。ほんとうにあの火それだわ。」

　「そうだ。見たまえ。そこらの三角標はちょうどさそり
の形にならんでいるよ。」

　ジョバンニはまったくその大きな火の向うに三つの三
角標がちょうどさそりの腕のようにこっちに五つの三角
標がさそりの尾やかぎのようにならんでいるのを見まし
た。そしてほんとうにそのまっ赤なうつくしいさそりの
火は音なくあかるくあかるく燃えたのです。

　その火がだんだんうしろの方になるにつれてみんなは
何とも言えずにぎやかなさまざまの楽の音や草花の<ruby>匂<rt>におい</rt></ruby>の
ようなもの口笛や人々のざわざわ言う声やらを聞きまし
た。それはもうじきちかくに町か何かがあってそこにお
祭でもあるというような気がするのでした。

　「ケンタウル露をふらせ。」いきなりいままで<ruby>睡<rt>ねむ</rt></ruby>ってい
たジョバンニのとなりの男の子が向うの窓を見ながら叫
んでいました。

for my own life 「一生
けん命」、一目散に

woe is me 「こんなに
なってしまった」、ああ悲
しいかな

in vain 「むなしく」

without so much
as a crackle 「音な
く」（without so much
as...: 〜もせずに）

murmur of voices
「ざわざわ言う声」、ざわめ
き

Outside the window stood a deep blue Christmas tree, a fir or cypress, its branches swimming with countless miniature bulbs, as if a thousand fireflies were swarming throughout them.

"How could I forget? Tonight was the Centaur Festival!"

"Yeah, this must be Centaur Village," piped in Campanella.

"Momentarily we will arrive at the Southern Cross," said the young man to the children. "Please prepare to alight."

"I'm gonna stay on the train a little bit longer," said Tadashi.

Kaoru stood up on shaky legs and made preparations to leave. She looked sad to have to say goodbye to Giovanni and Campanella.

"We must get off here," said the young man to Tadashi, closing his lips firmly.

"I won't! I'm gonna stay on a little longer!"

"You can stay on with us," said Giovanni, unable to hold himself in. "We've got a ticket that goes on forever!"

"But we have to get off here," said Kaoru, sadly. "This is where you get off to go to Heaven."

"Who says you have to go to Heaven? My teacher says that we have to create a place that's even better than Heaven."

"But our mummy's already there, and besides, God says so."

"A God who says that is a phony God."

ああそこにはクリスマストリイのようにまっ青な唐檜(とうひ)
かもみの木がたってその中にはたくさんのたくさんの豆
電燈がまるで千の蛍(ほたる)でも集ったようについていました。

「ああ、そうだ、今夜ケンタウル祭だねえ。」

「ああ、ここはケンタウルの村だよ。」カムパネルラが
すぐ言いました。〔以下原稿一枚？なし〕

「ボール投げなら僕決してはずさない。」*

男の子が大威張りで言いました。*

「もうじきサウザンクロスです。おりる支度をして下さ
い。」青年がみんなに言いました。

「僕も少し汽車へ乗ってるんだよ。」男の子が言いまし
た。カムパネルラのとなりの女の子はそわそわ立って支
度をはじめましたけれどもやっぱりジョバンニたちとわ
かれたくないようなようすでした。

「ここでおりなけぁいけないのです。」青年はきちっと
口を結んで男の子を見おろしながら言いました。

「厭(いや)だい。僕もう少し汽車へ乗ってから行くんだい。」

ジョバンニがこらえ兼ねて言いました。

「僕たちと一緒に乗って行こう。僕たちどこまでだって
行ける切符持ってるんだ。」

「だけどあたしたちもうここで降りなけぁいけないの
よ。ここ天上へ行くとこなんだから。」女の子がさびしそ
うに言いました。

「天上へなんか行かなくたっていいじゃないか。ぼくた
ちここで天上よりももっといいとこをこさえなけぁいけ
ないって僕の先生が言ったよ。」

「だっておっ母さんも行ってらっしゃるしそれに神さま
が仰(お)っしゃるんだわ。」

「そんな神さまうその神さまだい。」

fir 「もみ」

cypress ひのき

swarming 「集ったよう
に」、群れをなして

piped in 言葉を差しは
さんだ

* 「ボール投げなら僕決し
てはずさない。」

* 男の子が大威張りで言い
ました。

上記、原作のふたつの文は、
原作の原稿欠如により前後
の文脈の意味がつながらな
いため、英文では省略

phony 「うその」、偽物
の

"Your God is the phony one!"

"He is not!"

"What kind of God is your God?" interrupted the young man, smiling.

"How should I know?" said Giovanni. "But he's not like hers! He's the only real God."

"Of course the real God is only one," said the young man.

"I don't mean it that way," said Giovanni. "I mean the really real God."

"That's what I'm saying too. Let us pray that we will all meet someday in the course of time before that real God."

The young man humbly clasped his hands together, Kaoru did the same, and all of them looked frightfully pale and very reluctant to say goodbye to each other. Giovanni could hardly contain his tears.

"Well now, are you ready? We're nearly at the Southern Cross."

It was at that instant. Far downstream, there emerged, like a single tree out of the invisible water of the river, a cross studded with lights of blue, bitter orange and every color under the sun, crowned with a pale white halo of cloud. There was a great hustle and bustle inside the train as all the passengers stood to attention and prayed, just as they had done at the Northern Cross, and cries of joy, like the ones you hear when children reach for floating gourds, were heard, and deep pious sighs.

Eventually the cross came into full view outside the windows with the white halo cloud, whiter than the flesh of an apple, revolving ever so gently around it.

「あなたの神さまうその神さまよ。」

「そうじゃないよ。」

「あなたの神さまってどんな神さまですか。」青年は笑いながら言いました。

「ぼくほんとうはよく知りません、けれどもそんなんでなしにほんとうのたった一人の神さまです。」

「ほんとうの神さまはもちろんたった一人です。」

「ああ、そんなんでなしにたったひとりのほんとうのほんとうの神さまです。」

「だからそうじゃありませんか。わたくしはあなた方がいまにそのほんとうの神さまの前にわたくしたちとお会いになることを祈ります。」青年はつつましく両手を組みました。女の子もちょうどその通りにしました。みんなほんとうに別れが惜しそうでその顔いろも少し青ざめて見えました。ジョバンニはあぶなく声をあげて泣き出そうとしました。

「さあもう支度はいいんですか。じきサウザンクロスですから。」

ああそのときでした。見えない天の川のずうっと川下に青や橙やもうあらゆる光でちりばめられた十字架がまるで一本の木という風に川の中から立ってかがやきその上には青じろい雲がまるい環になって後光のようにかかっているのでした。汽車の中がまるでざわざわしました。みんなあの北の十字のときのようにまっすぐに立ってお祈りをはじめました。あっちにもこっちにも子供が瓜に飛びついたときのようなよろこびの声や何とも言ようない深いつつましいためいきの音ばかりきこえました。そしてだんだん十字架は窓の正面になりあの苹果の肉のような青じろい環の雲もゆるやかにゆるやかに繞っているのが見えました。

cross 「十字架」

studded with... 「～でちりばめられた」

hustle and bustle 喧騒、ざわざわした様子

pious 「つつましい」、敬虔な

"Hallelujah! Hallelujah!"

Their voices rang out pleasantly in chorus as they heard the crystal-clear call of a bugle from the remotest part of that cold remote sky. The train rolled slowly through a long series of signals and lamppost lights, crawling to an eventual stop directly in front of the cross.

"Well, everyone off!"

The young man took Tadashi's hand, making his way toward the exit.

"Goodbye for now," said Kaoru to the two boys, looking back at them.

"Goodbye," said Giovanni in a brusque voice, holding in his tears.

She looked back at them once more, her eyes wide open as if her heart was breaking in two, then silently left. The train was more than half empty, and before they knew it, there wasn't a soul left in it at all. A vacant wind blew through the wagons.

The boys looked outside. All of the people had come together, forming rows in humble prayer, kneeling on the shore of the Milky Way in front of the cross. A holy figure in a white robe was crossing the invisible water, coming toward them with outstretched arms.

But at that very moment, the glass whistle blew, the train inched forward, and a silver mist came streaming up between them and the river. Nothing was visible there now save for a grove of walnut trees, their leaves gleaming, and a cute little electric squirrel with a golden halo who kept poking his face through the mist.

「ハルレヤハルレヤ。」明るくたのしくみんなの声はひびきみんなはそのそらの遠くからつめたいそらの遠くからすきとおった何とも言えずさわやかなラッパの声をききました。そしてたくさんのシグナルや電燈の灯のなかを汽車はだんだんゆるやかになりとうとう十字架のちょうどま向いに行ってすっかりとまりました。

「さあ、下りるんですよ。」青年は男の子の手をひきだんだん向うの出口の方へ歩き出しました。

「じゃさよなら。」女の子がふりかえって二人に言いました。

「さよなら。」ジョバンニはまるで泣き出したいのをこらえて怒ったようにぶっきり棒に言いました。女の子はいかにもつらそうに眼を大きくしても一度こっちをふりかえってそれからあとはもうだまって出て行ってしまいました。汽車の中はもう半分以上も空いてしまい俄かにがらんとしてさびしくなり風がいっぱいに吹き込みました。

そして見ているとみんなはつつましく列を組んであの十字架の前の天の川のなぎさにひざまずいていました。そしてその見えない天の川の水をわたってひとりの神々しい白いきものの人が手をのばしてこっちへ来るのを二人は見ました。けれどもそのときはもう硝子の呼子は鳴らされ汽車はうごき出しと思ううちに銀いろの霧が川下の方からすうっと流れて来てもうそっちは何も見えなくなりました。ただたくさんのくるみの木が葉をさんさんと光らしてその霧の中に立ち黄金の円光をもった電気栗鼠が可愛い顔をその中からちらちらのぞいているだけでした。

---

crystal-clear 「すきとおった」

bugle 「ラッパ」

brusque ぶっきらぼうな、不愛想な

wagons （鉄道）貨車

inched forward じりじりと前進した、少しずつ進んだ

poking his face 顔をのぞかせる

When the mist finally began to lift they could see a wide road lined with electric lights skirting the track for some distance then leading off into the blue. The little pea-colored lights blipped off as the train approached, as if acknowledging its presence, then blipped back on again as it passed.

The cross had shrunk so small in the distance that it looked like you could pick it right up and hang it on your chest, and there was no way on earth of knowing whether the little girl, the young man and the others were still kneeling on that white shore or had already gone off somewhere to their heaven.

"Campanella," said Giovanni, sighing deeply, "we're alone again. Let's stay together till the ends of the earth, okay? If I could be like that scorpion and do something for the benefit of all people, I wouldn't care if my body burnt up a hundred times over."

"Me too," said Campanella, his eyes welling with the clearest tears.

"But what is real happiness, Campanella?"

"Search me," he answered dreamily.

"We'll keep our spirits up, won't we?" said Giovanni, taking a deep breath and feeling a new strength gushing through him.

そのときすうっと霧がはれかかりました。どこかへ行く街道らしく小さな電燈の一列についた通りがありました。それはしばらく線路に沿って進んでいました。そして二人がそのあかしの前を通って行くときはその小さな豆いろの火はちょうど挨拶でもするようにぽかっと消え二人が過ぎて行くときまた点くのでした。

ふりかえって見るとさっきの十字架はすっかり小さくなってしまいほんとうにもうそのまま胸にも吊されそうになり、さっきの女の子や青年たちがその前の白い渚にまだひざまずいているのかそれともどこか方角もわからないその天上へ行ったのかぼんやりして見分けられませんでした。

ジョバンニはああと深く息しました。

「カムパネルラ、また僕たち二人きりになったねえ、どこまでもどこまでも一緒に行こう。僕はもうあのさそりのようにほんとうにみんなの幸のためならば僕のからだなんか百ぺん灼いてもかまわない。」

「うん。僕だってそうだ。」カムパネルラの眼にはきれいな涙がうかんでいました。

「けれどもほんとうのさいわいは一体何だろう。」ジョバンニが言いました。

「僕わからない。」カムパネルラがぼんやり言いました。

「僕たちしっかりやろうねえ。」ジョバンニが胸いっぱい新らしい力が湧くようにふうと息をしながら言いました。

Search me 「僕わからない」。この部分については解説 p.13 を参照。

pea-colored 「豆いろ」

blipped off... blipped back on 「ぽかっと消え～また点く」

welling with... 「（涙が）うかんで」、～が湧き出て

gushing through 湧き出る、ほとばしる

"Hey, there's the Coal Sack!" cried Campanella, pointing to a spot in the Milky Way and leaning back as he did so. "It's a hole in the sky!"

Giovanni was flabbergasted as he peered down into the Coal Sack. It was a huge black gaping hole in the river, and the longer he stared and squinted into it, the more his eyes smarted and he couldn't tell how deep the bottom went or what was down below it.

"I'm not scared of all that dark," he said. "I'm going to get to the bottom of everything and find out what will make people happy. We'll go together, Campanella, as far as we can go."

"Yes we will, Giovanni. Oh," cried Campanella, pointing to a distant field, "that's the most beautiful field I have ever seen. Everybody's there. That's the real heaven. Look, my mother's there too. Look!"

Giovanni looked, but what he saw was all milky white and blurry, not at all like what Campanella was describing. He felt indescribably lonely as he peered out, catching sight only of two telegraph poles on the opposite bank, their red crossbeams aligned like linking arms.

「あ、あすこ石炭袋だよ。そらの孔だよ。」カムパネル
ラが少しそっちを避けるようにしながら天の川のひとと
こを指さしました。ジョバンニはそっちを見てまるでぎ
くっとしてしまいました。天の川の一とこに大きなまっ
くらな孔がどおんとあいているのです。その底がどれほ
ど深いかその奥に何があるかいくら眼をこすってのぞい
てもなんにも見えずただ眼がしんしんと痛むのでした。
ジョバンニが言いました。

　「僕もうあんな大きな暗の中だってこわくない。きっと
みんなのほんとうのさいわいをさがしに行く。どこまで
もどこまでも僕たち一緒に進んで行こう。」

　「ああきっと行くよ。ああ、あすこの野原はなんてきれ
いだろう。みんな集ってるねえ。あすこがほんとうの天
上なんだ。あっあすこにいるのぼくのお母さんだよ。」カ
ムパネルラは俄かに窓の遠くに見えるきれいな野原を指
して叫びました。

　ジョバンニもそっちを見ましたけれどもそこはぼん
やり白くけむっているばかりどうしてもカムパネルラが
言ったように思われませんでした。何とも言えずさびし
い気がしてぼんやりそっちを見ていましたら向うの河岸
に二本の電信ばしらが丁度両方から腕を組んだように赤
い腕木をつらねて立っていました。

Coal Sack 「石炭袋」。
コールサックとは、南十字
座付近に見ることができる
暗黒星雲で、一部はケンタ
ウルス座とはえ座に重なる

flabbergasted 「ぎ
くっとして」、面食らった

gaping hole ぽっかり
開いた穴

smarted 「しんしんと
痛む」、ズキズキと痛んだ、
うずいた

peered out じっと見
つめた

crossbeams 「腕木」、
横梁

"Campanella," said Giovanni, turning toward him, "we're going to stick together, okay?"

But there was no Campanella where Campanella had been sitting, only the black shining velvet seat. Giovanni bolted up like a rocket, leaning far out the window so that he wouldn't be heard as he screamed into the sky, pounding his chest hard and crying out with a throat full of tears.

Everything seemed to go black at once.

Giovanni opened his eyes. He had fallen asleep, exhausted, in the grass on the hill. He felt a strange burning sensation inside as cold tears streamed down his cheeks, and he sprang to his feet.

The town below was bound together by countless lights just as before, yet now they were somehow more radiant mellow. The Milky Way, where he had just dreamt himself to, was still a hazy blurry white mass smoking above the black southern horizon, with the red star in Scorpio twinkling beautifully to the right beside it. The stars in the sky did not appear to have changed position very much from before.

Giovanni sprinted down the hill. All he could think of was his mother who was waiting until he came home before having her dinner. He passed through the black grove of pine trees, turned by the faintly white pasture fence and came to the front entrance of the darkened cowshed. It looked like someone was in now, because he saw a cart with two barrels of something loaded on it.

"Hello, anybody here?" shouted Giovanni.

「カムパネルラ、僕たち一緒に行こうねえ。」ジョバンニがこう言いながらふりかえって見ましたらそのいままでカムパネルラの座っていた席にもうカムパネルラの形は見えずただ黒いびろうどばかりひかっていました。ジョバンニはまるで鉄砲丸のように立ちあがりました。そして誰にも聞えないように窓の外へからだを乗り出して力いっぱいはげしく胸をうって叫びそれからもう咽喉いっぱい泣きだしました。もうそこらが一ぺんにまっくらになったように思いました。

　ジョバンニは眼をひらきました。もとの丘の草の中につかれてねむっていたのでした。胸は何だかおかしく熱り頬にはつめたい涙がながれていました。

　ジョバンニはばねのようにはね起きました。町はすっかりさっきの通りに下でたくさんの灯を綴ってはいましたがその光はなんだかさっきよりは熱したという風でした。そしてたったいま夢であいた天の川もやっぱりさっきの通りに白くぼんやりかかりまっ黒な南の地平線の上では殊にけむったようになってその右には蠍座の赤い星がうつくしくきらめき、そらぜんたいの位置はそんなに変ってもいないようでした。

　ジョバンニは一さんに丘を走って下りました。まだ夕ごはんをたべないで待っているお母さんのことが胸いっぱいに思いだされたのです。どんどん黒い松の林の中を通ってそれからほの白い牧場の柵をまわってさっきの入口から暗い牛舎の前へまた来ました。そこには誰かがいま帰ったらしくさっきなかった一つの車が何かの樽を二つ乗っけて置いてありました。

　「今晩は、」ジョバンニは叫びました。

bolted up　急に立ち上がった

sprang to his feet
「はね起きました」

mellow　熟した、（音、光などが）柔らかい

cowshed　「牛舎」

barrels　「樽」

"Coming!"

A man in heavy white pants emerged, adding, "What can I do for you?"

"Well, we didn't get our milk delivered today."

"Oh, I'm terribly sorry."

The man immediately went in back and returned with a bottle of milk.

"Really sorry about this," he said, handing the bottle to Giovanni and smiling. "This afternoon I was pretty careless and left the gate to the calf pen open. The little devil made a beeline to his mother and drank up half her milk."

"I see. Well, I'll take this home then."

"Please do. Terribly sorry about this."

"That's fine."

Giovanni went out the pasture gate with both hands wrapped around the warm bottle of milk. He walked a distance through a heavily treed part of town, coming out onto the main road, and when he reached the crossroad, he could see to his right the turrets of the big bridge standing tall in the hazy sky over the river where Campanella and the others had gone to float lanterns.

Small groups of women who had gathered on the corners of the crossroad and in front of the shops were looking toward the bridge and speaking in hushed tones. The bridge itself was swimming in all kinds of light.

Giovanni, feeling a strange chill inside, shouted to the people close by, "Is something wrong?"

「はい。」白い太いずぼんをはいた人がすぐ出て来て立ちました。

「何のご用ですか。」

「今日牛乳がぼくのところへ来なかったのですが」

「あ済みませんでした。」その人はすぐ奥へ行って一本の牛乳瓶（ぎゅうにゅうびん）をもって来てジョバンニに渡しながらまた言いました。

「ほんとうに、済みませんでした。今日はひるすぎうっかりしてこうしの柵をあけて置いたもんですから大将早速親牛のところへ行って半分ばかり呑（の）んでしまいましてね……」その人はわらいました。

「そうですか。ではいただいて行きます。」

「ええ、どうも済みませんでした。」

「いいえ。」

ジョバンニはまだ熱い乳の瓶（びん）を両方のてのひらで包むようにもって牧場の柵（さく）を出ました。

そしてしばらく木のある町を通って大通りへ出てまたしばらく行きますとみちは十文字になってその右手の方、通りのはずれにさっきカムパネルラたちのあかりを流しに行った川へかかった大きな橋のやぐらが夜のそらにぼんやり立っていました。

ところがその十字になった町かどや店の前に女たちが七八人ぐらいずつ集って橋の方を見ながら何かひそひそ談（はな）しているのです。それから橋の上にもいろいろなあかりがいっぱいなのでした。

ジョバンニはなぜかさあっと胸が冷たくなったように思いました。そしていきなり近くの人たちへ

「何かあったんですか。」と叫ぶようにききました。

emerged 「出て来た」、現れて

calf pen 「こうしの柵」、仔牛の囲い

made a beeline to... ～へまっすぐに行った、～に直行した

in hushed tones 「ひそひそ」

swimming in... 「～がいっぱい」、～であふれる

chill 冷たさ、寒気

"A child has fallen into the water," said one of them, as they all turned at once toward him.

Giovanni ran for his life toward the bridge. The river was invisible for all of the people on the bridge. A policeman in white was among them.

Giovanni reached the end of the bridge and flew down to a wide section of the river. Many lights were moving up and down along the water's edge, and a number of lantern flames could be seen roving the dark embankment on the opposite bank as well. Between them the river, with no lantern to illuminate it now, flowed in a single gray tranquil stream with little more than a murmur. People were standing in a black mass at the farthest point downstream where the river formed a sandbar. Giovanni quickly made his way there, bumping into Marceau, who had been with Campanella earlier.

"Giovanni," said Marceau, running up. "Campanella's fallen into the river."

"Why? When?"

"Zanelli was trying to push a lantern down the river from the boat, and that's when the boat tilted and kind of dumped him into the water. Campanella dove right in after him and he pushed Zanelli back to the boat, and Kato got ahold of him, but then nobody could see Campanella after that."

"But everybody's looking, aren't they?"

"Yeah, they all came right away, Campanella's father too. But nobody can find him. They took Zanelli home."

「こどもが水へ落ちたんですよ。」一人が言いますとその人たちは一斉にジョバンニの方を見ました。ジョバンニはまるで夢中で橋の方へ走りました。橋の上は人でいっぱいで河が見えませんでした。白い服を着た巡査も出ていました。

ジョバンニは橋の袂<ruby>袂<rt>たもと</rt></ruby>から飛ぶように下の広い河原へおりました。

その河原の水際に沿ってたくさんのあかりがせわしくのぼったり下ったりしていました。向う岸の暗いどてにも火が七つ八つうごいていました。そのまん中をもう<ruby>烏<rt>からす</rt></ruby><ruby>瓜<rt>うり</rt></ruby>のあかりもない川が、わずかに音をたてて灰いろにしずかに流れていたのでした。

河原のいちばん下流の方へ<ruby>州<rt>す</rt></ruby>のようになって出たところに人の集りがくっきりまっ黒に立っていました。ジョバンニはどんどんそっちへ走りました。するとジョバンニはいきなりさっきカムパネルラといっしょだったマルソに会いました。マルソがジョバンニに走り寄ってきました。

「ジョバンニ、カムパネルラが川へはいったよ。」

「どうして、いつ。」

「ザネリがね、舟の上から烏うりのあかりを水の流れる方へ押してやろうとしたんだ。そのとき舟がゆれたもんだから水へ落っこったろう。するとカムパネルラがすぐ飛びこんだんだ。そしてザネリを舟の方へ押してよこした。ザネリはカトウにつかまった。けれどもあとカムパネルラが見えないんだ。」

「みんな探してるんだろう。」

「ああすぐみんな来た。カムパネルラのお父さんも来た。けれども見附からないんだ。ザネリはうちへ連れられてった。」

roving うろつく、さまよう

embankment 「どて」

tranquil 静かな、穏やかな

sandbar 「州」、砂洲

Giovanni went to where everyone was milling about. Campanella's father, wearing a black suit, his jaw angular and pale, was staring at the watch gripped in his right hand. He stood tall, encircled by students and townspeople.

Everyone's eyes were fixed on the river. Not a soul was saying a word. Giovanni's legs trembled and quaked. The ripples of the black water flashed and sparkled as acetylene lamps roamed over the river, just like at fishing time.

Downstream, the Milky Way was reflected from one edge of the river to the other as if there was no water there at all but only sky. Giovanni felt that by now Campanella could be nowhere but on the very farthest edge of that river that was only sky.

But everyone still wanted to believe that from somewhere among the waves Campanella would appear and say, "Boy, did I ever swim!" … or that he would be standing on a sandbar that the people didn't even know existed, waiting for someone to find him.

All of a sudden Campanella's father spoke up emphatically.

"It's no use. It's been forty-five minutes since he fell in."

ジョバンニはみんなの居るそっちの方へ行きました。そこに学生たち町の人たちに囲まれて青じろい尖（とが）ったあごをしたカムパネルラのお父さんが黒い服を着てまっすぐに立って右手に持った時計をじっと見つめていたのです。

みんなもじっと河を見ていました。誰（たれ）も一言も物を言う人もありませんでした。ジョバンニはわくわくわくわく足がふるえました。魚をとるときのアセチレンランプがたくさんせわしく行ったり来たりして黒い川の水はちらちら小さな波をたてて流れているのが見えるのでした。

下流の方は川はば一ぱい銀河が巨（おお）きく写ってまるで水のないそのままのそらのように見えました。

ジョバンニはそのカムパネルラはもうあの銀河のはずれにしかいないというような気がしてしかたなかったのです。

けれどもみんなはまだ、どこかの波の間から、

「ぼくずいぶん泳いだぞ。」と言いながらカムパネルラが出て来るか或（ある）いはカムパネルラがどこかの人の知らない洲（す）にでも着いて立っていて誰かの来るのを待っているかというような気がして仕方ないらしいのでした。けれども俄（にわ）かにカムパネルラのお父さんがきっぱり言いました。

「もう駄目（だめ）です。落ちてから四十五分たちましたから。」

milling about 　ひしめいている

angular 　「尖った」

soul 　（否定文で）「誰も」（いない）

trembled and quaked 　「ふるえました」

acetylene lamps 　「アセチレンランプ」。炭化カルシウムと水を反応させ、発生したアセチレンガスを燃焼することで明るい光を発する照明器具

roamed over 　「行ったり来たりして」

emphatically 　「きっぱり」

Giovanni raced up and stood before him. I know where Campanella went. I traveled with Campanella. That's what he wanted to say, but the words just stuck somewhere in his throat.

Campanella's father, thinking that Giovanni had come to offer his sympathy, peered for some time straight into his eyes and said politely ...

"You would be Giovanni, isn't that right? Thank you for coming tonight, son."

Giovanni bowed, unable to speak.

"Has your father come back home yet?" he asked, still gripping the watch in his fist.

"No," replied Giovanni with a slight shake of his head.

"I wonder what could have happened? Just two days ago I had a wonderful letter from him. He should be home by about today. The boat must have been delayed, that's it. You'll come to our home tomorrow after school with everyone else, won't you, Giovanni?"

With those words Campanella's father gazed far downstream where the galaxy was part of the river itself.

Giovanni had no words for the many feelings that filled his heart. He left Campanella's father and went home to take the milk to his mother and tell her about his father's homecoming, running as fast as his legs would take him along the river's edge toward town.

ジョバンニは思わずかけよって博士の前に立って、ぼくはカムパネルラの行った方を知っていますぼくはカムパネルラといっしょに歩いていたのですと言おうとしましたがもうのどがつまって何とも言えませんでした。すると博士はジョバンニが挨拶^{あいさつ}に来たとでも思ったものですか、しばらくしげしげジョバンニを見ていましたが

　「あなたはジョバンニさんでしたね。どうも今晩はありがとう。」と叮^{てい}ねいに言いました。

　ジョバンニは何も言えずにただおじぎをしました。

　「あなたのお父さんはもう帰っていますか。」博士は堅く時計を握ったまままたききました。

　「いいえ。」ジョバンニはかすかに頭をふりました。

　「どうしたのかなあ。ぼくには一昨日^{おととい}大へん元気な便りがあったんだが。今日あたりもう着くころなんだが。船が遅れたんだな。ジョバンニさん。あした放課後みなさんとうちへ遊びに来てくださいね。」

　そう言いながら博士はまた川下の銀河のいっぱいにうつった方へじっと眼を送りました。

　ジョバンニはもういろいろなことで胸がいっぱいでなんにも言えずに博士の前をはなれて早くお母さんに牛乳を持って行ってお父さんの帰ることを知らせようと思うともう一目散に河原を街の方へ走りました。

offer his sympathy
追悼の意を表す、お悔やみを述べる

インドラの網
Indra's Net

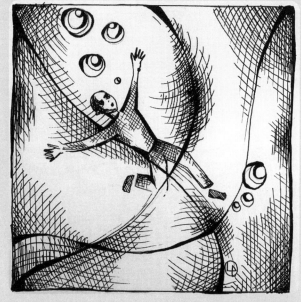

イラスト：ルーシー・バルバース

Indra's Net を読むまえに

天の空間を感じとる

インドラの網の向こうに広がる空間と光景を想像しながら、
この美しい小品を味わってみよう。

🔊 **10**　*p.*146/150-162

　『インドラの網』は、賢治の最も美しい散文詩です。すべての光を忠実に、そして完全に反射する完璧なダイヤモンドのような作品だと思います。そして、この小品は宮沢賢治の心のありようのメタファーにもなっています。

　あるひとりの旅人（作品の中では「私」と表現されています）が今まで慣れ親しんだ世界から遠く離れたところにいることに気づきます。旅人は完全に疲労困憊している状態です。この旅人は誰で、今どこにいるのでしょうか。

　青木晃と名乗るこの旅人は、偉大な于闐大寺を発掘した人物だといいます。「青木晃」は賢治の作品の登場人物にいかにもふさわしい名前です。賢治の作品で最もよく使われる色は青だからです。青は空の色であり、異世界への入り口であり、異世界の象徴でもあります。

　また、賢治は「何と云はれても」(p.183)という詩の中で、自分自身を「ひかる水玉」であると書いています。賢治が選んだ「晃」の字は、「輝く」という意味もあり、日の出を連想させます。

　于闐は、新疆ウイグル自治区の砂漠地帯にあります。1896年から1910年にかけて、探検家のスヴェン・ヘディンとオーレル・スタインが、紀元前2世紀から1200年までの遺物を発掘した場所です。

　しかし、青木は于闐から遠く離れた場所にいます。青木がいるのはインド北部のヒマラヤ山脈にある標高4,000メートルを越えるツェラ高原です。青木(＝賢治)はそのような高い場所に立って楽園を臨んでいます。そこは「インドラの網」の向こうにある楽園であり、力強く打ち鳴らされた太鼓が静まり返る場所であり、速い動きが止まり、マイナスの太陽が闇を放射する場所でもあります。そのような光景全体が、すべてが混

沌としていながら辻褄があって、明確で完璧な意味を持っています。

インドラは、日本語では「帝釈天」と呼ばれていますが、インドのウッタラカンド州にある標高6,600mのメルー峰の山頂に居を構えています。そこには、仏陀や菩薩も住んでいます。インドラは、この聖なる家の上空に無限の網を張っているのです。

「インドラの網」は、それ自体が宇宙のあらゆるものをつないでいます。そのようにこの「網」という言葉は、「私たちが見たり感じたりするものはすべてつながっていて、そのつながりこそが道徳的な人生観の基礎になる」と確信していた賢治にとってのうってつけのメタファーです。空間や時間、国籍や民族、宗教がどんなに離れていても、私たちは皆、お互いの運命を共有しています。私が考えていること、やっていることが相手に影響を与えますし、その逆もまた然りです。私たちは生まれながらに「一蓮托生」なのです。

しかし、青木は困惑します。

「こいつはやっぱりおかしいぞ」と彼は思います。「天の空間は私の感覚のすぐ隣りに居るらしい」。

賢治は、心の内側の風景が、現実の外側の風景と「隣り合わせ」にあり、融け合っていることを教えてくれます。賢治は「『春と修羅』序」の中で、自分自身を「ひとつの青い照明」「すべてわたくしと明滅し／みんなが同時に感ずるもの」(p.185)と表現しています。糸状の「インドラの網」によって、宇宙のすべてと私はそれぞれ互いの一部となるのです。

「インドラの網」にかかった子どもたちは、この物語で最も魅力的なキャラクターです。ガンダーラにおける天使のような存在です。

太陽がまもなく昇ります。

「光は針や束になってそそぎそこらいちめんかちかち鳴りました。」

賢治の光の描写は無数にありますが、「針や束になってそそぎ」というこの言葉は、絶妙な叙情性と科学的な正確さを兼ね備えていると思います。賢治が亡くなったのは、ちょうど量子力学の理論が広まった頃ですが、光子が電磁場の量子であれば、「束」はその量子に実によく似ています。

「インドラの網」の中の天人の衣は、ガンダーラの彫像のように、ひだが流れているようで動いていません。天人は一瞬で数百キロの距離を移動することができるのです。

この広大で混沌とした宇宙で、私たち個人の苦しみに何の意義があるのか——この疑問は、賢治を生涯悩ませました。死とは恐れるべきものなのでしょうか。

賢治はこの問いに、『ひかりの素足』という作品の中で、仏陀の言葉として見事に答えています。

「おまえたちの罪はこの世界を包む大きな徳の力にくらべれば、太陽の光とあざみの棘のさきの小さな露のようなもんだ。なんにもこわいことはない。」

宮沢賢治はその「死は恐れるべきものなのか」という疑問に答えるために、青木晃の身を借りて地の果てまで行ったのです。仏陀の『ひかりの素足』の中の言葉以上に、希望と喜びと光に満ちた、これ以上的確な答えを、私は考えることはできません。

It seemed then that I had collapsed, out of utter exhaustion, on a bed of green grass and wind.

In that faint of autumn wind, I exchanged bows, courteous to a fault, with my tin-colored shadow.

Then, I stepped alone onto a dark cowberry carpet and traveled about the Tsela Plateau.

The cowberry boasted red fruit.

The white sky blanketed the entire plateau. It was a cold white, whiter than kaolin china.

The rarefied air sang in a high-pitched whirr, no doubt due to the sun making its lonely way beyond the white porcelain clouds. The sun had already sunk below the black barbed ridges in the west, creaking in the dim light of a late afternoon.

I looked around, gasping like a fish.

Wherever I looked, there wasn't even a shadow of a bird, nor was there so much as a trace of any gentle beast.

"What on earth am I visiting here in the upper reaches of the atmosphere, moving around in this air that cuts through me?"

I asked this of myself.

The cowberry was, before I knew it, gone, and the ground was covered in a sheet of dry ash-colored moss. Red moss flowers were blossoming here and there. But all this did was to intensify the cold grief of the plateau.

Before long, the late afternoon was in twilight, the moss flowers appeared reddish black, and the color of the sky above the ridges turned a faint and somber yellow.

It was then that I caught sight of an all-white lake far in the distance.

そのとき私は大へんひどく疲れていてたしか風と草穂との底に倒れていたのだとおもいます。

その秋風の昏倒の中で私は私の錫いろの影法師にずいぶん馬鹿ていねいな別れの挨拶をやっていました。

そしてただひとり暗いこけももの敷物を踏んでツェラ高原をあるいて行きました。

こけももには赤い実もついていたのです。

白いそらが高原の上いっぱいに張って高陵産の磁器よりもっと冷たく白いのでした。

稀薄な空気がみんみん鳴っていましたがそれは多分は白磁器の雲の向うをさびしく渡った日輪がもう高原の西を劃る黒い尖尖の山稜の向うに落ちて薄明が来たためにそんなに軋んでいたのだろうとおもいます。

私は魚のようにあえぎながら何べんもあたりを見まわしました。

ただ一かけの鳥も居ず、どこにもやさしい獣のかすかなけはいさえなかったのです。

（私は全体何をたずねてこんな気圏の上の方、きんきん痛む空気の中をあるいているのか。）

私はひとりで自分にたずねました。

こけももがいつかなくなって地面は乾いた灰いろの苔で覆われところどころには赤い苔の花もさいていました。けれどもそれはいよいよつめたい高原の悲痛を増すばかりでした。

そしていつか薄明は黄昏に入りかわられ、苔の花も赤ぐろく見え西の山稜の上のそらばかりかすかに黄いろに濁りました。

そのとき私ははるかの向うにまっ白な湖を見たのです。

courteous to a
fault 「馬鹿ていねいな」
（courteous 丁寧な / to
a fault 過剰に、過度に）

cowberry コケモモ

the Tsela Plateau
「ツェラ高原」。北インドのタワング地区と西カメン地区に位置する標高 4170m の高原で、仏教の町タワングとディランを結び、グワーハーティーへと続く

blanketed 一面を覆った

rarefied air 「稀薄な空気」

barbed とげのある

somber yellow くすんだ黄色

"That's not water! It's natrium salt or something that's crystallized," I said to myself. "I mustn't lose heart by getting all content and taken in."

Even so, I hurried over there.

The lake came closer, glittering. Before I knew it, I was gazing at pure-white quartz sand and, beyond that, a place brimming darkly with real water.

The sand squeaked. I picked up a pinch of it and examined it in the dim light of the sky. It was made up of dihexagonal pyramid grains.

"This has come from dacite or rhyolite."

That's what I figured, whispering to myself, standing on the water's edge.

"Hey, this is supercooled water!" I whispered in my mind. "This is the granddaddy of water in both a liquid and a solid state!"

My palm absolutely gave off a pale phosphorescence in the water.

Suddenly there was a high-pitched ring all around.

"It's the wind. It's the spears of grass. Thundering!" These were the words ringing in my head. It was pitch dark, pitch dark with a faint tinge of red.

I opened my eyes wider.

Night had fallen and the sky was as transparent as it could ever be. The water of the galaxy flowed silently over the sky's plain which was made of beautifully fired polished steel. Little corundum pebbles shined; and every grain of sand on the banks could be counted.

（水ではないぞ、また曹達（ソーダ）や何かの結晶だぞ。いまのうちひどく悦（よろこ）んで欺（だま）されたとき力を落しちゃいかないぞ。）私は自分で自分に言いました。

それでもやっぱり私は急ぎました。

湖はだんだん近く光ってきました。間もなく私はまっ白な石英の砂とその向うに音なく湛（たた）えるほんとうの水とを見ました。

砂がきしきし鳴りました。私はそれを一つまみとって空の微光にしらべました。すきとおる複六方錐（ふくろくほうすい）の粒だったのです。

（石英安山岩か流紋岩から来た。）

私はつぶやくようにまた考えるようにしながら水際に立ちました。

（こいつは過冷却の水だ。氷相当官なのだ。）私はも一度こころの中でつぶやきました。

全く私のてのひらは水の中で青じろく燐光（りんこう）を出していました。

あたりが俄（にわか）にきいんとなり、

（風だよ、草の穂だよ。ごうごうごうごう。）こんな語（ことば）が私の頭の中で鳴りました。まっくらでした。まっくらで少しうす赤かったのです。

私はまた眼を開きました。

いつの間にかすっかり夜になってそらはまるですきとおっていました。素敵に灼（や）きをかけられてよく研かれた鋼鉄製の天の野原に銀河の水は音なく流れ、鋼玉の小砂利も光り岸の砂も一つぶずつ数えられたのです。

taken in　だまされる

brimming darkly　「音なく湛える」（darkly 神秘的に、ひそかに / brimming 溢れだしそうな）

dihexagonal pyramid　「複六方錐」

dacite　デイサイト。火成岩の一種で、深成岩の花崗閃緑岩にあたる

rhyolite　「流紋岩」。深成岩である花崗岩と同等である成分の火山岩の一種

gave off (give off)　放つ

phosphorescence　「燐光」。物質が光を発する現象、またはその発する光の全般。

spears　芽、若葉

corundum　「鋼玉」。酸化アルミニウムの結晶からなる鉱物。

The cold dark-violet plate of the sky was studded with the cleavage planes of diamonds and pointy grains of sapphire; and fragments of citrine the size of smoke bush seeds had been picked up in exquisite tweezers and inlaid into it; and all of this separately and on its own breathed in and out, trembling and quaking.

When I took another look at where my feet were, small yellow and blue flames were flickering and twinkling in the grains of sand in the sky. I suppose that supercooled lake in the Tsela Plateau was a part of the galaxy itself.

Yet, dawn seemed to come quickly on the plateau.

It was very clear that something like glassy molecules you could see right through were floating up into the air; and, above all, what looked like a fountain in the sky surrounded by nine small blue stars in the east was quickly transformed in the terribly dim light of the sky from steel to amazonite.

I saw an angel fly through space that had a dark-violet, subtle sheen.

"At last it's slipped in," I thought, my heart jumping with delight. "It has suddenly made its way from the Tsela Plateau of the realm of humans to that of the heavens."

The angel soared straight ahead.

"It's covering more than a thousand kilometers in the blink of an eye!" I whispered to myself. "But look! It isn't even budging. It's soaring ahead so far without moving, without changing place, without changing form."

The angel's robe was as thin as smoke, and its holy necklace absorbed whispers of light from the dimly-lit plate of the sky.

またその桔梗いろの冷たい天盤には金剛石の劈開片や青宝玉の尖った粒やあるいはまるでけむりの草のたねほどの黄水晶のかけらまでごく精巧のピンセットできちんとひろわれきれいにちりばめられそれはめいめい勝手に呼吸し勝手にぷりぷりふるえました。

　私はまた足もとの砂を見ましたらその砂粒の中にも黄いろや青や小さな火がちらちらまたたいているのでした。恐らくはそのツェラ高原の過冷却湖畔も天の銀河の一部と思われました。

　けれどもこの時は早くも高原の夜は明けるらしかったのです。

　それは空気の中に何かしらそらぞらしい硝子の分子のようなものが浮んで来たのでもわかりましたが第一東の九つの小さな青い星で囲まれたそらの泉水のようなものが大へん光が弱くなりそこの空は早くも鋼青から天河石の板に変っていたことから実にあきらかだったのです。

　その冷たい桔梗色の底光りする空間を一人の天が翔けているのを私は見ました。

　（とうとうまぎれ込んだ、人の世界のツェラ高原の空間から天の空間へふっとまぎれこんだのだ。）私は胸を躍らせながらこう思いました。

　天人はまっすぐに翔けているのでした。

　（一瞬百由旬を飛んでいるぞ。けれども見ろ、少しも動いていない。少しも動かずに移らずに変らずにたしかに一瞬百由旬ずつ翔けている。実にうまい。）私はこうつぶやくように考えました。

　天人の衣はけむりのようにうすくその瓔珞は昧爽の天盤からかすかな光を受けました。

studded　ちりばめられた

cleavage planes　「劈開片」、劈開面

citrine　「黄水晶」

smoke bush　「けむりの草」、カスミノキ。ウルシ科の落葉小高木。開花後に花柄が糸のように長く伸びて、全体が柔らかな羽毛状になる様子から、英名も smoke tree や smoke bush（煙の草）と呼ばれる

inlaid　はめ込まれた

amazonite　「天河石」、アマゾナイト。緑色のケイ酸塩鉱物で、発色は鉛によるもの

soared　飛翔した、舞い上がった

a thousand kilometers　原作の「由旬」は古代インドにおける長さの単位。書籍あるが、1由旬をおよそ10キロメートルと考えると、「百由旬」は1000キロメートル。

angel's robe　「天人の衣」

"Got it," I thought. "The air here is rarefied almost to the point of becoming a vacuum. That's why there's no wind disturbing the folds in that delicate robe."

The angel opened its dark blue eyes wide but didn't blink them once. It soared absolutely straight ahead with the faintest smile on its lips. Yet, it was neither moving, nor changing place or form.

"This is the place where all aspirations are purified. The number of wishes is submerged. Gravity is neutralized within itself, and a cold scent of quince floats through the air. And so, the cord on the angel's robe neither ripples, nor does it hang straight down."

But then the amazonite in the sky was transformed into a weird plate of purple agate, and I could no longer see the figure of the soaring angel.

"This is the Tsela Plateau after all," I said, explaining it to myself. "You can't count on just one single episode of blending."

But what was strange was that the cold quince-like scent was still permeating the sky. And once again I sensed that this mysterious world in the sky was like a dream.

"There's something really puzzling here!" I thought to myself, standing there. "This celestial space seems to be right beside my sensations. As I walk on the path here and fragments of mica gradually appear in great number, it seems to me that I am getting closer and closer to granite. It may be just a fluke, but the more often it appears this way, the truer it gets. I'm sure I'll be able to sense this celestial world on this plateau again."

（ははあ、ここは空気の稀薄が殆んど真空に均しいのだ。だからあの繊細な衣のひだをちらっと乱す風もない。）私はまた思いました。

天人は紺いろの瞳を大きく張ってまたたき一つしませんでした。その唇は微かに晒いまっすぐにまっすぐに翔けていました。けれども少しも動かず移らずまた変りませんでした。

（ここではあらゆる望みがみんな浄められている。願いの数はみな寂められている。重力は互に打ち消され冷たいまるめろの匂いが浮動するばかりだ。だからあの天衣の紐も波立たずまた鉛直に垂れないのだ。）

けれどもそのとき空は天河石からあやしい葡萄瑪瑙の板に変りその天人の翔ける姿をもう私は見ませんでした。

（やっぱりツェラの高原だ。ほんの一時のまぎれ込みなどは結局あてにならないのだ。）こう私は自分で自分に誨えるようにしました。けれどもどうもおかしいことはあの天盤のつめたいまるめろに似たかおりがまだその辺に漂っているのでした。そして私はまたちらっとさっきのあやしい天の世界の空間を夢のように感じたのです。

（こいつはやっぱりおかしいぞ。天の空間は私の感覚のすぐ隣りに居るらしい。みちをあるいて黄金いろの雲母のかけらがだんだんたくさん出て来ればだんだん花崗岩に近づいたなと思うのだ。ほんのまぐれあたりでもあんまり度々になるととうとうそれがほんとになる。きっと私はもう一度この高原で天の世界を感ずることができる。）私はひとりでこう思いながらそのまま立って居りました。

aspirations 願望

submerged 沈められた、呑まれた、抑えられた

quince 「まるめろ」、マルメロ。西洋かりんとも呼ばれ、よい香りがある

agate 「瑪瑙」

permeating 浸透している、染み込んでいる

celestial 空の、天界の

fragments of mica 「雲母のかけら」

granite 「花崗岩」。深成岩の一種

fluke 「まぐれあたり」、思わぬ幸運

I turned my eyes from the sky to the plateau. The sand was now as pure white as can be. The blue of the lake, now more ancient-looking than verdigris, gave my heart a chill.

Suddenly I saw three heavenly children before me. They wore the thinnest robes, woven, it seemed, from frost, and transparent shoes, standing on the water's edge, peering intently into the eastern sky, as if waiting for the sun to rise. The eastern sky was already alight with whiteness. From the folds in their robes I could tell they were from Gandhara. I recognized them as being from a fresco that I had excavated at the ruins of the great Khotan Temple. I approached them quietly and greeted them in a very low voice, so as not to frighten them.

"Good morning, children of the fresco at the great Khotan Temple."

The three of them turned toward me. Ah, the radiance of their holy necklaces and their imposing and magnificent black eyes!

I spoke again, continuing to approach them.

"Good morning, children of the fresco at the great Khotan Temple."

"And who may you be?" asked the child on the right, looking straight at me without blinking.

"I am Aoki Akira, who excavated the great Khotan Temple from beneath the sands."

"And what are you doing here?" said the same child, looking sternly at me straight in the eye.

"I want to worship the sun together with you."

そして空から瞳を高原に転じました。全く砂はもうまっ白に見えていました。湖は緑青よりももっと古びその青さは私の心臓まで冷たくしました。

ふと私は私の前に三人の天の子供らを見ました。それはみな霜を織ったような羅をつけすきとおる沓をはき私の前の水際に立ってしきりに東の空をのぞみ太陽の昇るのを待っているようでした。その東の空はもう白く燃えていました。私は天の子供らのひだのつけようからそのガンダーラ系統なのを知りました。またそのたしかに于闐大寺の廃趾から発掘された壁画の中の三人なことを知りました。私はしずかにそっちへ進み愕かさないようにごく声低く挨拶しました。

「お早う、于闐大寺の壁画の中の子供さんたち。」

三人一緒にこっちを向きました。その瓔珞のかがやきと黒い厳めしい瞳。

私は進みながらまた言いました。

「お早う。于闐大寺の壁画の中の子供さんたち。」

「お前は誰だい。」

右はじの子供がまっすぐに瞬もなく私を見て訊ねました。

「私は于闐大寺を沙の中から掘り出した青木晃というものです。」

「何しに来たんだい。」少しの顔色もうごかさずじっと私の瞳を見ながらその子はまたこう言いました。

「あなたたちと一緒にお日さまをおがみたいと思ってです。」

verdigris 「緑青」
Gandhara 「ガンダーラ」。現在のパキスタン西北部に位置する
excavated 発掘した
Khotan Temple 「于闐大寺」。于闐は古代、中国の西域にあったオアシス都市国家
without blinking 「瞬もなく」
Aoki Akira 「青木晃」。この名前については p.147 参照。
radiance 「かがやき」
imposing 「厳めしい」、印象的な、堂々とした
sternly 「少しの顔色も動かさず」、厳格に、厳しく
worship 拝む、崇拝する

"The sun? It won't be long for you to wait."

The three of them turned away from me. Their necklaces briefly shined like yellow and bitter-orange and green needles, and their robes fluttered in the colors of the rainbow.

In the fiery platinum sky, from the edge of the olive-green field beyond the lake, something that looked like it was melted, something seductive, as old as gold, crimson like that seen in a kiln, a single ray of light appeared.

The heavenly children stood perfectly erect and brought their hands together, looking toward it.

It was the sun. It was the sun of this heavenly realm, solemnly rocking its strangely round body that was like a thing melted down, in an instant climbing properly up in the sky. Its light now flowed in needles and bundles, and everywhere you looked you could hear a clicking and clacking.

The heavenly children jumped up and down in rapture, running over the silica sand of the pure-blue lake of True Enlightenment. Then suddenly one of the children bumped into me, and jumping back, screamed out while pointing up to the sky.

"Look, look, look at Indra's net!"

I looked up at the sky. The zenith was now azure blue, and from it to the four corners of the pale edges of the sky, Indra's spectral net vibrated radiantly as if burning, its fibers more fine than a spider's web, its construction more elaborate than that of hypha, all blending together transparently, purely, in a billion intermingled parts.

「そうですか。もうじきです。」三人は向うを向きました。瓔珞は黄や橙や緑の針のようなみじかい光を射、羅は虹のようにひるがえりました。

　そして早くもその燃え立った白金のそら、湖の向うの鶯いろの原のはてから熔けたようなもの、なまめかしいもの、古びた黄金、反射炉の中の朱、一きれの光るものが現われました。

　天の子供らはまっすぐに立ってそっちへ合掌しました。

　それは太陽でした。厳かにそのあやしい円い熔けたようなからだをゆすり間もなく正しく空に昇った天の世界の太陽でした。光は針や束になってそそぎそこらいちめんかちかち鳴りました。

　天の子供らは夢中になってはねあがりまっ青な寂静印の湖の岸、硅砂の上をかけまわりました。そしていきなり私にぶっつかりびっくりして飛びのきながら一人が空を指して叫びました。

　「ごらん、そら、インドラの網を。」

　私は空を見ました。いまはすっかり青ぞらに変ったその天頂から四方の青白い天末までいちめんはられたインドラのスペクトル製の網、その繊維は蜘蛛のより細く、その組織は菌糸より緻密に、透明清澄で黄金でまた青く幾億互に交錯し光って顫えて燃えました。

fiery platinum sky
「燃え立った白金のそら」

seductive 　「なまめかしい」、魅惑的な

kiln 　「炉」、窯

brought their hands together 　「合掌しました」

heavenly realm 　「天の世界」、天界

solemnly 　「厳かに」

in rapture 　「夢中になって」、うっとりして

True Enlightenment 「寂静印」。涅槃寂静印とは、「涅槃寂静」という世界があるという真理が説かれている仏教の旗印で、「涅槃寂静」とは、苦しみが滅して救われた世界のこと

zenith 　「天頂」

azure blue 　瑠璃色

hypha 　「菌糸」

intermingled 　混じった、混ぜられた

インドラの網　161

"Look, heavens, it's the drums of the wind!" said another child, bumping into me and running off in a flurry.

What can only be seen as the sun's minus counterpart shined indigo dark and gold and green and ashen, and drums seemed to drop from the sky, and, impervious to human striking, pounded out a sound with all their might; and while those countless heavenly drums called out, they seemed to be making no sound at the same time. I watched it all for so long that my eyes clouded over and all I could do was stagger about.

"Look, look at the blue peacock!" quietly said the same child who was on the right as he walked by me.

Sure enough, beyond Indra's net in the sky, on the far edge of those countless resounding heavenly drums, an enormous and strange blue peacock, fanning out its jeweled train, sang out in an ethereal voice. That peacock was most certainly present in the sky. Yet, it was not to be seen at all. It was certainly crying out. Yet its cries were not to be heard at all.

After that, there was no way that I could see the three heavenly children.

Far from it, I vaguely recalled my own figure collapsed deep into the green grass and the hollows of the wind.

「ごらん、そら、風の太鼓。」も一人がぶっつかってあわてて遁げ（に）ながらこう言いました。ほんとうに空のところどころマイナスの太陽ともいうように暗く藍（あい）や黄金（きん）や緑や灰いろに光り空から陥（お）ちこんだようになり誰（たれ）も敲（たた）かないのにちからいっぱい鳴っている、百千のその天の太鼓は鳴っていながらそれで少しも鳴っていなかったのです。私はそれをあんまり永く見て眼も眩（くら）くなりよろよろしました。

「ごらん、蒼孔雀（あおくじゃく）を。」さっきの右はじの子供が私と行きすぎるときしずかにこう言いました。まことに空のインドラの網のむこう、数しらず鳴りわたる天鼓のかなたに空一ぱいの不思議な大きな蒼い孔雀が宝石製の尾ばねをひろげかすかにクウクウ鳴きました。その孔雀はたしかに空には居りました。けれども少しも見えなかったのです。たしかに鳴いて居りました。けれども少しも聞えなかったのです。

そして私は本当にもうその三人の天の子供らを見ませんでした。

却（かえ）って私は草穂と風の中に白く倒れている私のかたちをぼんやり思い出しました。

in a flurry　慌ただしく

impervious to...　〜の影響を受けずに

stagger about　よろよろと動き回る

fanning out　扇形に広がって

ethereal　軽やかに、この世のものと思えない

hollows　隙間、空洞

マグノリアの木
The Magnolia Tree

イラスト：ルーシー・パルバース

The Magnolia Tree を読むまえに

春の道場

僧侶の諒安がやってきた山の中のマグノリアの花が咲き乱れる地は、修行の場でもある。そこで諒安（＝賢治）は何を見て何を悟ったのだろうか。

🔊 11 *p.164-178*

賢治の人生には、「もう死ぬかもしれない」と思った時期が何度もありました。肺が弱く、疲れやすく、結核性胸膜炎にもかかりました。息をするのも苦しいときに、黒い手帳に鉛筆で書き留めたのが、後に彼の代表作となる「雨ニモマケズ」です。この詩を書いたのは1931年11月3日のことで、手帳の最初のページの一番上に「11.3」と書かれています。

私がこの詩を初めて読んだのは1968年はじめのことで、「11.3」というタイトルが付けられていました。その詩が正式に「雨ニモマケズ」と呼ばれるようになったのは、それから数年後のことです。

1929年の春、賢治は病床に伏していました。咳き込むと口から血が出ました。彼の詩「夜」には1929年4月28日の日付があり、その中で彼は「樹などしづかに息してめぐむ春の夜……」と語っています。そして、彼は次のように書いています。

こゝこそ春の道場で
菩薩は億の身をも棄て
諸仏はこゝに涅槃し住し給ふ故

「春の道場」という言葉は、この『マグノリアの木』の中にも出てきます。私はここでこの言葉を the training ground of spring と訳しています。

この地は、僧侶である諒安がやってきた場所です。諒安は悟りを求めてやってきたのだろうと思われます。この作品に描かれた世界は、彼の修行の場であり、そこから解脱して涅槃の世界に入る道を見出すかもしれない場所なのです。

このマグノリアの花びらの香りは、詩的な祈りを漂わせています。自然は賢治と交信し、自らを悟ることが成仏する道であることを教えてく

れています。

　諒安は賢治の分身であり、もう一人の自分でもあり、旅は賢治自身の内面への旅なのです。

　「これがお前の世界なのだよ」と誰かが叫ぶ。諒安本人かもしれない。「お前に丁度当たり前の世界なのだよ。それよりももっとほんとうはこれがお前の中の景色なのだよ」(*p.*169)

　賢治は、物語や詩の中で、旅人たちのことをしばしば書いています。旅人は疲れ果て、草の上に横たわって眠り、気がつくと別世界にいます。

　諒安は、自分が山を颯爽と登っていく姿を見ます。山の平らかな場所に着くと、一本のモクレンの木があり、その両脇に二人の子どもがいるのが見えます。しかし、この子どもたちは諒安とは別の存在ではありません。子どもたちもまた、自分たちは諒安であることを告げます。それは、諒安が子どもたちを感じ取ることができるからです。賢治の思想によると、私たちは他者を感じ、その思考や感情を共有することで、他者になます。このことが、他者への深い共感と献身を生み出す源になります。私たちは皆、感覚によって、意識によって、互いにつながっているのです。

　物語の最後にわかるように、すべての善と悪は絡み合っています。飢饉や疫病などを含むすべての現象の因果関係は、自然や人類の本質の一部です。ここでキーワードとなるのが、「しのびをならう（忍を習う）」です。私はしばらく、この概念を理解するのに苦労しました。しかし、賢治は、人間が忍耐や寛容を「実行」することを説いているのだと気づいていました。「忍」の意味は、「困難や迫害に立ち向かう忍耐力、忍辱」です。悪意に直面しても憎まず、暴力や飢餓、疫病などの苦難に直面しても屈せず、「忍」を身につけることを賢治は望んでいます。これは「雨

ニモマケズ」と同じメッセージで、他人の苦しみを自分の苦しみとしてとらえ、それを軽減するために行動すること、悪を愛で否定するものです。

　この物語に登場するマグノリアの木は、Magnolia Grandiflora St. Maryで、日本では「サンタ・マグノリア」といわれています。アメリカ南東部に自生し、クリーム色の大きな花びらが特徴です。しかし、賢治がこの名前を物語に使ったのは、イエスの母にちなんでのことではないでしょうか。『マグノリアの木』の舞台はインドのヒマラヤ地方と思われ、マグノリア・チャンパカが生育し、崇拝されています。その花は黄色か白で、とても香りが良いので、この木の別名は「喜びの香木」と呼ばれています。また、Magnolia Kobusは日本では「コブシ」として知られ、賢治が親しんだ木で、日本原産です。実は、マグノリアの木は諒安の魂が映し出された鏡のようなものなのですが、それらのマグノリアがすべてがひとつになったものなのでしょう。

　　　これは賢治の詩「夜」の最後の一節です。

こんやもうこゝで誰にも見られず
ひとり死んでもいゝのだと
いくたびさうも考をきめ
自分で自分に教へながら
またなまぬるく
あたらしい血が湧くたび
なほほのじろくわたくしはおびえる

　賢治が春の道場へと向かう鍵は、賢治自らが手を引いて自分自身を導いていることです。そして、マグノリアの木のそばで、諒安（賢治）はこの世とあの世を垣間見ているのです。

A damp and gloomy fog hung over everything.

Ryoan was making his way under the blanket of fog, tramping up and down the steep slopes of the valley. He plodded on and on, the sole of his shoe half worn through, from peaks that reached to the heavens to the darkest deepest bottom of valleys, and once again upwards to the next towering cliff, swallowed up in fog.

The thought occurred to him that, if it was possible to swim through that fog, he would sail like the wind from one cliff straight to another. As it was, he had no choice but to trudge up the precipitous punishing surfaces of these monstrous sculptures then down again to the flatter planes below, his body burning as he panted for breath, crawling over the earth.

Black jagged boulders whistled in the freezing fog. Though feeling desolate and totally alone, he put his heart and soul into trekking up and down. Even the huge clump of little blackish shrubs growing in the depths of the valley looked cruel the way they absorbed all the light around them. And yet, this did not deter Ryoan, who continued all by himself on his way from one notched peak to the next.

No sooner did the fog suddenly glow with a dim light than it slid back into half darkness. This occurred again and again. The dim whitish light would simply not give in to night.

Ryoan came to a gently sloping area where lustrous snake's beard blanketed the ground. He threw himself down, dozed off and was soon dead to the world.

"This is your world, you know. This is the world that suits you down to the ground. But really, more than that, it's the landscape inside you, you know."

霧がじめじめ降っていた。

諒安は、その霧の底をひとり、険しい山谷の、刻みを渉って行きました。

杳の底を半分踏み抜いてしまいながらそのいちばん高い処からいちばん暗い深いところへまたその谷の底から霧に吸いこまれた次の峯へと一生けんめい伝って行きました。

もしもほんの少しのはり合で霧を泳いで行くことができたら一つの峯から次の巌へずいぶん雑作もなく行けるのだが私はやっぱりこの意地悪い大きな彫刻の表面に沿ってけわしい処ではからだが燃えるようになり少しの平らなところではほっと息をつきながら地面を這わなければならないと諒安は思いました。

全く峯にはまっ黒のガツガツした巌が冷たい霧を吹いてそらうそぶき折角いっしんに登って行ってもまるでよるべもなくさびしいのでした。

それから谷の深い処には細かなうすぐろい灌木がぎっしり生えて光を通すことさえも慳貪そうに見えました。

それでも諒安は次から次とそのひどい刻みをひとりわたって行きました。

何べんも何べんも霧がふっと明るくなりまたうすくらくなりました。

けれども光は淡く白く痛く、いつまでたっても夜にならないようでした。

つやつや光る竜の髭のいちめん生えた少しのなだらに来たとき諒安はからだを投げるようにしてとろとろ睡ってしまいました。

（これがお前の世界なのだよ、お前に丁度あたり前の世界なのだよ。それよりもっとほんとうはこれがお前の中の景色なのだよ。）

magnolia　モクレン。*p.175*の「ほおの木」も同じもの（*p.167*の解説参照）

plodded　とぼとぼと歩いた、ゆっくり進んだ

trudge up　一生懸命に上る、重い足取りで上る

precipitous　急勾配の、断崖絶壁の

panted for breath　あえいだ、息を切らした

jagged　ぎざぎざの

boulder　「巌」、巨礫

deter　妨げる、思いとどませる

give in to　受け入れる、屈する

lustrous　光沢のある、ぴかぴかした

snake's beard　「竜の髭（リュウノヒゲ）」。「蛇の髭（ジャノヒゲ）」ともいう。キジカクシ科の多年草。細長い葉が地面を覆うように茂る

Someone, or maybe Ryoan himself, was screaming that over and over again not far from his ear.

"That's right, that's right, that's absolutely right. This is obviously my landscape. It's me. So there's not much I can do about it," replied Ryoan, nodding off.

"The seductive clump ...
The training ground of spring
Where you learn
To treat all
Without malice"

The voice could clearly be heard coming from somewhere. Ryoan opened his eyes. The chilling fog permeated his entire body. The fog was now so white that it hurt the eyes, and the blue slope of snake's beard glimmered faintly inside it.

Ryoan dashed down the mountain. But he caught his foot in one of the shrubs and tumbled to the ground. He stood up, a wry smile on his lips. A precipice of small trees appeared suddenly before his eyes. He climbed up it, clinging to the branches of those spicewood trees. The spicewood trees sent a faint fragrance into the fog, and the fog afforded Ryoan something soft smooth and milky white in return. Ryoan smiled as he clawed his way up the side of the mountain.

It was then that the fog turned all gloomy, and Ryoan threw it that faint smile of his. At that, the fog brightened up again.

誰かが、或いは諒安自身が、耳の近くで何べんもこう叫んでいました。

（そうです。そうです。そうですとも。いかにも私の景色です。私なのです。だから仕方がないのです。）諒安はうとうとこう返事しました。

（これはこれ

惑う木立の

中ならず

しのびをならう

春の道場）

どこからかこんな声がはっきり聞えて来ました。諒安は眼をひらきました。霧がからだにつめたく浸み込むのでした。

全く霧は白く痛く竜の髯の青い傾斜はその中にぼんやりかすんで行きました。諒安はとっとっとかけ下りました。

そしてたちまち一本の灌木に足をつかまれて投げ出すように倒れました。

諒安はにが笑いをしながら起きあがりました。

いきなり険しい灌木の崖が目の前に出ました。

諒安はそのくろもじの枝にとりついてのぼりました。くろもじはかすかな匂を霧に送り霧は俄かに乳いろの柔らかなやさしいものを諒安によこしました。

諒安はよじのぼりながら笑いました。

その時霧は大へん陰気になりました。そこで諒安は霧にそのかすかな笑いを投げました。そこで霧はさっと明るくなりました。

The training ground of spring 「春の道場」。解説の *p*.165 参照

learn to treat all without malice 「しのびをならう」。解説の*p*.166 参照

seductive 「惑う」、誘惑的な、なやましい

wry smile 苦笑い

precipice 崖

spicewood trees 「くろもじ」。クロモジ属はクスノキ科の落葉低木で、枝と葉は薬用になる

Finally, he reached a plateau of withered grass. Standing there, he felt all warm and golden, and he sensed that the faint odor of sweat was leaving his body in thin threads, surging up into the fog. A single spectacular black horse emerged, prancing out of that thought, then disappearing into the fog.

The fog, in an instant, pitched and rolled, and Ryoan caught sight of something that looked like floating amber molecules, glittering brightly. In a flash those amber molecules were gleaming gold, then fresh green, pelting down like the rains.

Ryoan's dim shadow fell onto the withered grass. A sliver of his fragrant odor flashed and glistened, traveling straight through the suspension of that fog and amber-green mass. But before he knew it, the whole scene was drenched in gold again.

The fog melted away. The sun swayed like a liquid, to and fro, in the newly polished azurite sky, and the bright wax of unmelted fog that did remain dripped down, here and there, into the valley.

"Ah, that's where I've just been, that awful sheer valley. But what a spectacular sight this is! And, let me see, there's that, too!"

Ryoan didn't believe his eyes. In the countless crags of the valley, sheets of white magnolia flowers were blooming, silver in color when struck by the sun, more like snow where not.

"Enveloping the steeply notched
Cliffs on the heart ...
Could it be young magnolia flowers?"

This voice from somewhere could clearly be heard. Ryoan took in the scene with a heart full of light.

そして諒安はとうとう一つの平らな枯草の頂上に立ちました。

そこは少し黄金いろでほっとあたたかなような気がしました。

諒安は自分のからだから少しの汗の匂いが細い糸のようになって霧の中へ騰って行くのを思いました。その汗という考から一疋の立派な黒い馬がひらっと躍り出して霧の中へ消えて行きました。

霧が俄かにゆれました。そして諒安はそらいっぱいにきんきん光って漂う琥珀の分子のようなものを見ました。それはさっと琥珀から黄金に変りまた新鮮な緑に遷ってまるで雨よりも滋く降って来るのでした。

いつか諒安の影がうすくかれ草の上に落ちて居ました。一きれのいいかおりがきらっと光って霧とその琥珀との浮遊の中を過ぎて行きました。

と思うと俄かにぱっとあたりが黄金に変りました。霧が融けたのでした。太陽は磨きたての藍銅鉱のそらに液体のようにゆらめいてかかり融けのこりの霧はまぶしく蠟のように谷のあちこちに澱みます。

（ああこんなけわしいひどいところを私は渡って来たのだな。けれども何というこの立派さだろう。そしてはてな、あれは。）

諒安は眼を疑いました。そのいちめんの山谷の刻みにいちめんまっ白にマグノリアの木の花が咲いているのでした。その日のあたるところは銀と見え陰になるところは雪のきれと思われたのです。

（けわしくも刻むこころの峯々に　いま咲きそむるマグノリアかも。）こう言う声がどこからかはっきり聞えて来ました。諒安は心も明るくあたりを見まわしました。

withered grass　枯草

surging up　こみ上げる、沸き起こる

prancing out　「躍り出して」、（馬などが）踊り跳ねる

pitched and rolled　揺れる、動揺する

drenched in gold　黄金にてらされて

azurite　藍銅鉱。炭酸塩鉱物の一種で、ブルー・マラカイトと呼ばれる宝石

sheer　険しい、切り立った

crags　ごつごつした岩石、険しい岩山

There was a single tall magnolia tree standing not far in the distance, with two children on either side of its trunk.

"Ah, it was those children who were singing a moment ago. But wait ... they're not just plain kids."

Ryoan took a really good look at them. They were like a dream in a fasting dawn, dressed in gossamer and sacred raiments, glittering in the light of the sun. But it seems that the song had not been sung by them. That's because one of the children had been singing in a thin voice from long before that, glaring up to the very top of the magnolia tree.

"Santa Magnolia
Shining bright to the tips
Of your every branch"

The child on the other side replied ...

"Silver dove soaring
To the heavens"

The first child sang again ...

"Heavenly dove descending
From the heavens"

Ryoan quietly continued on his way.

"The magnolia tree stands for the peacefulness of Nirvana. Where are we?"

"We don't know that," answered one of the children humbly, raising its bright eyes.

すぐ向うに一本の大きなほおの木がありました。その下に二人の子供が幹を間にして立っているのでした。

（ああさっきから歌っていたのはあの子供らだ。けれどもあれはどうもただの子供らではないぞ。）諒安はよくそっちを見ました。

その子供らは羅をつけ瓔珞をかざり日光に光り、すべて断食のあけがたの夢のようでした。ところがさっきの歌はその子供らでもないようでした。それは一人の子供がさっきよりずうっと細い声でマグノリアの木の梢を見あげながら歌い出したからです。

「サンタ、マグノリア、
　枝にいっぱいひかるはなんぞ。」

向う側の子が答えました。

「天に飛びたつ銀の鳩。」

こちらの子がまたうたいました。

「セント、マグノリア、
　枝にいっぱいひかるはなんぞ。」

「天からおりた天の鳩。」

諒安はしずかに進んで行きました。

「マグノリアの木は寂静印です。ここはどこですか。」

「私たちにはわかりません。」一人の子がつつましく賢こそうな眼をあげながら答えました。

gossamer 「羅」、薄くて軽い生地

raiments 衣服

Nirvana 「寂静印」、涅槃。涅槃とは、ヒンドゥー教、ジャイナ教、仏教において、輪廻から解放された状態のこと

humbly 「つつましく」、謙虚に

"Yes, the magnolia tree is Nirvana."

The unwavering clear voice came to Ryoan from behind. He quickly turned around. A man just like him, dressed like the children, was standing perfectly straight alongside them.

"Was it you singing back there before?"

"Yes, me. But it's also you. If you want to know why, it's because you can sense me."

"Yes, I can ... thank you ... it's me ... and it's also you. It's because, whatever is me is also in you."

The man laughed. The two of them bowed lightly to each other for the first time.

"It's really so flat here," said Ryoan, gazing at the beautiful golden grassy plateau behind him.

"Yes," said the man, smiling, "it is flat. But the flat here is only flatness in comparison with the steepness. It's not a real flatness."

"That's right. It's flat because of the steep mountains I climbed to get here."

"Look! Those steep mountains are covered in magnolia blossoms."

"I see. Thank you. So, then, the magnolia is where all afflictions and negative feelings are obliterated. Those petals are softer than the goat's milk of Paradise. Its fragrance wafts exalted poetic prayer to those who have attained Enlightenment."

"It is all goodness itself."

「そうです、マグノリアの木は寂静印です。」

　強いはっきりした声が諒安のうしろでしました。諒安は急いでふり向きました。子供らと同じなりをした丁度諒安と同じくらいの人がまっすぐに立ってわらっていました。

「あなたですか、さっきから霧の中やらでお歌いになった方は。」

「ええ、私です。またあなたです。なぜなら私というものもまたあなたが感じているのですから。」

「そうです、ありがとう、私です、またあなたです。なぜなら私というものもまたあなたの中にあるのですから。」

　その人は笑いました。諒安（りょうあん）と二人ははじめて軽く礼をしました。

「ほんとうにここは平らですね。」諒安はうしろの方のうつくしい黄金（きん）の草の高原を見ながら言いました。その人は笑いました。

「ええ、平らです、けれどもここの平らかさはけわしさに対する平らさです。ほんとうの平らさではありません。」

「そうです。それは私がけわしい山谷を渡ったから平らなのです。」

「ごらんなさい、そのけわしい山谷にいまいちめんにマグノリアが咲いています。」

「ええ、ありがとう、ですからマグノリアの木は寂静です。あの花びらは天の山羊（やぎ）の乳よりしめやかです。あのかおりは覚者（かくしゃ）たちの尊い偈（げ）を人に送ります。」

「それはみんな善です。」

afflictions　試練、苦悩、難儀

obliterated　消し去る、抹消する

wafts　（風などに乗って）ふわりと運ぶ、漂わせる

exalted　「尊い」、高尚な、高貴な

Enlightenment　「正覚」。正覚とは、仏教用語で真の悟りのことを指す。

goodness　「善」

"Whose goodness?" asked Ryoan, taking a last look at the magnolia on the golden plateau and the steep faces of the mountains.

"The goodness of the Enlightened."

His shadow fell, purple and transparent, into the grass.

"Yes ... and it is our goodness, too. The goodness of the Enlightened is absolute. It appears in the magnolia tree, as it does in the cold boulders of the steep cliffs. The dark dense forests of the valleys and the rivers flowing on and on and the frequent revolutions and famines and epidemics that occur where those rivers flood ... all is the goodness of the Enlightened. But here, the magnolia tree is the goodness of the Enlightened and, at the same time, our own."

The two of them bowed again, respectfully, to each other.

イラスト：ルーシー・バルバース

「誰の善ですか。」諒安はも一度その美しい黄金の高原とけわしい山谷の刻みの中のマグノリアとを見ながらたずねました。

「覚者の善です。」その人の影は紫いろで透明に草に落ちていました。

「そうです、そしてまた私どもの善です。覚者の善は絶対です。それはマグノリアの木にもあらわれ、けわしい峯のつめたい巌にもあらわれ、谷の暗い密林もこの河がずうっと流れて行って氾濫をするあたりの度々の革命や饑饉や疫病やみんな覚者の善です。けれどもここではマグノリアの木が覚者の善でまた私どもの善です。」

諒安とその人と二人はまた恭しく礼をしました。

Enlightened 「覚者」。覚者とは、仏教用語で真理を体得し悟りを得た人のこと

famines 饑饉

epidemics 疫病

『春と修羅』序
Preface to Spring and Ashura

イラスト：ルーシー・バルバース

Preface to Spring and Ashura を読むまえに

光の記録係

詩集『春と修羅』の副題は「心象スケッチ」。賢治は自らの詩を「心象スケッチ」と呼んだが、これは何を意味しているのだろうか。

🔊 **12** *p.180-188*

宮沢賢治は、人生における自分の役割のひとつは「光の記録係」であると考えていたと思います。鳥類学者が鳥を研究し分類するように、宇宙学者が銀河を研究するように、賢治は光の兆候を観察し、記録し、分類し、研究しました。そして、さらにもう一歩踏み込んで、自分自身を「ひとつの青い照明」であると表現したのです。賢治は自分自身を、光を放ち反射する宇宙のあらゆるものから切り離された存在だとは考えていませんでした。

賢治は自分の詩を「心象スケッチ」と呼びましたが、このことも「『春と修羅』序」に反映されています。しかし、「心象スケッチ」という言葉は一体何を意味しているのでしょうか。

賢治は、私たちが感覚を通して現実を処理していることを知っていました。つまり、現実そのものは、私たちが共通して感じていることにほかならないのです。これは彼の現象学とでもいうべきものの本質的な要素であります。賢治が書いたり描いたりするもののすべては、見たもの、聞いたもの、嗅いだもの、味わったもの、感じたもののスケッチにほかならないのです。ここでいう「心象」とは、「現実から想像されるもの」という意味です。アートには、現実自体というものはありません。現実に見えるものとそうでないものがあるだけです。

賢治は、mental sketch modifiedという英語も使っています。ここでのmodifiedは、「変形された」とか「構成された」という意味です。つまり、インクと紙を使って、自分の心象を言葉として変化させ、適応させ、再度記述していることを意味しています。また、ノートの中でmental sketch revivedという英語のタームも出てきます。言い換えれば、「再生された心象スケッチ」となります。これは、彼の創作物が現実から取り出され、想像の中で作り直され、文学や芸術として「再生された」、「復

活された」ことを意味しています。宮沢賢治という人間は、現実と芸術的創造をつなぐ媒介で、観察し、記録し、再現しているにすぎないのです。

　この奇跡の詩で再現された現実は、時間的にも空間的にも流動的なものです。地質学のような学問でさえも、思われるほど地に足がついているものではありません。絶えず変化し続ける賢治の世界では、数百年後、川や山は別の場所にあり、今は空気であるものが海になっているかもしれません。賢治にとって常にあの世への入り口である青空は、「無色な孔雀」であふれているかもしれません。賢治が仏教から借りてきたこの孔雀は、毒草や虫を食べ、それを美しい色に変える能力を持つ、畏敬すべき美徳と善のシンボルです。つまり、賢治にとって孔雀は、自分の体の中にあるあらゆる心の悩みや苦しみの痕跡を消し去ってくれる比喩的存在なのです。だから、賢治は孔雀に習って、私たちは他人の苦しみや悩みをすべて自分の中に吸収すべきだと考えています。

　賢治はこの詩の内容を「命題」と呼んでいます。賢治は後世に残すために「再生された心象スケッチ」を行い、日付を入れる現実の記録者なのです。「命（いのち）」と「題（だい）」（問題、テーマ）からなるこの「命題」という言葉は、まさに宮沢賢治にふさわしい言葉と言えるでしょう。

　「『春と修羅』序」は、賢治が自らの人生のテーマについて最も明晰に語ったものであるにちがいありません。

「詩ノート」の中にある賢治の詩「何と云はれても」を紹介します。この詩に見ることができるのは、賢治自身のアイデンティティーの自己定義で、彼の全作品の中での大切な自画像です。

何と云はれても	**Whatever Anyone Says**
何と云はれても	Whatever anyone says
わたくしはひかる水玉	I am the young wild olive tree
つめたい雫	Dripping radiant dew
すきとほった雨つぶを	Cold droplets
枝いっぱいにみてた	Transparent rain
若い山ぐみの木なのである	From my every branch

この短い詩は、きちんと「である」で終わる一文です。科学者の賢治は、自分自身を木として想像しているぐらい、自然を明晰に、そして親密に描写しています。そのように描くことは、人から見ればきっとおかしいと思われるかもしれないことを賢治は承知しています。しかし、賢治は人からどう言われようが気にしません。彼は自分自身が自然の不可分の一部であると見なしていたからです。なお、この詩の「みてた」は「満ちた」の意味です。

イラスト：ルーシー・パルバース

Preface to Spring and Ashura

The phenomenon called I
Is a single blue illumination
Of a presupposed organic alternating current lamp
(a composite body of each and every transparent specter)
The single illumination
Of karma's alternating current lamp
Remains alight without fail
Flickering unceasingly, restlessly
Together with the sights of the land and all else
(the light is preserved ... the lamp itself is lost)

These poems are a mental sketch formed faithfully
Passage by passage of light and shade
Maintained and preserved to this point
Brought together in paper and mineral ink
From the directions sensed as past
For these twenty-two months
(the totality flickers in time with me
all sensing all that I sense)

春と修羅 序

わたくしといふ現象は
仮定された有機交流電燈の
ひとつの青い照明です
　　（あらゆる透明な幽霊の複合体）
風景やみんなといつしよに
せはしくせはしく明滅しながら
いかにもたしかにともりつづける
因果交流電燈の
ひとつの青い照明です
　　（ひかりはたもち　その電燈は失はれ）

これらは二十二箇月の
過去とかんずる方角から
紙と鉱質インクをつらね
　　（すべてわたくしと明滅し
　　みんなが同時に感ずるもの）
ここまでたもちつゞけられた
かげとひかりのひとくさりづつ
そのとほりの心象スケツチです

preface　序文、前書き
Ashura　阿修羅。略して修羅ともいう。元々はインド神話においてはインドラ神と対抗する悪神、鬼神。仏教においては仏法を守護する八部衆の一人
presupposed　「仮定された」、想定された、前提の
composite body　「複合体」
specter　「幽霊」、亡霊
passage by passage　「ひとくさりづつ」
totality　「すべて」、全体

People and galaxies and ashura and sea urchins
Will think up new ontological proofs as they see them
Consuming their cosmic dust … breathing in salt water and air
In the end all of these make up a landscape of the heart
I assure you, however, that the scenes recorded here
Are scenes recorded solely in their natural state
And if this is nihil then it is nothing but nihil
And the totality is common in degree to all of us
(just as everything forms what is the sum in me
so do all parts become the sum of everything)

These words were meant to be transcribed truthfully
In the monstrous bright accumulation of time
Of the present geological era
Yet they have gone ahead and altered their construct and
     quality
In what amounts to a mere point of contrasted light
(or alternatively a billion years of ashura)
Now it is possible that both the printer and I
Have been sharing a certain turn of mind
Causing us to sense these as unaltered
In all probability just as we are aware of our own sense organs
And of scenery and of people through feeling
And just as what is is but what we sense in common
So it is that documents and history … or the Earth's past
Are nothing but what we have become conscious of
Along with their diverse data
(at the root of the karmic qualifications of space-time)

これらについて人や銀河や修羅や海胆は
宇宙塵をたべ　または空気や塩水を呼吸しながら
それぞれ新鮮な本体論もかんがへませうが
それらも畢竟こゝろのひとつの風物です
たゞたしかに記録されたこれらのけしきは
記録されたそのとほりのこのけしきで
それが虚無ならば虚無自身がこのとほりで
ある程度まではみんなに共通いたします
　（すべてがわたくしの中のみんなであるやうに
　みんなのおのおののなかのすべてですから）

けれどもこれら新生代沖積世の
巨大に明るい時間の集積のなかで
正しくうつされた筈のこれらのことばが
わづかその一点にも均しい明暗のうちに
　　　（あるいは修羅の十億年）
すでにはやくもその組立や質を変じ
しかもわたくしも印刷者も
それを変らないとして感ずることは
傾向としてはあり得ます
けだしわれわれがわれわれの感官や
風景や人物をかんずるやうに
そしてたゞ共通に感ずるだけであるやうに
記録や歴史　あるいは地史といふものも
それのいろいろの論料《データ》といつしよに
　（因果の時空的制約のもとに）
われわれがかんじてゐるのに過ぎません

sea urchins 「海胆」、
うに
ontological proof
「本体論」的証明。神は最
も完全なものであり、その
完全性には存在も含まれて
いなければならないため、
神は存在するという論法
nihil 「虚無」。ニヒリズ
ムあるいは虚無主義とは、
今生きている世界における
人間の存在には、意義、目
的や理解できるような真理
などがないという哲学的主
張
monstrous 巨大な
the present
geological era 「新生
代沖積世」。「沖積世」とは、
地質時代区分の区分のうち
で最も新しい時代で、約
一万年前から近未来を含む
現在までを指す
turn of mind 気立て、
気質

For all I know in two thousand years from now
An appropriately different geology will be applied
With fitting proofs revealed one after another from the past
And everyone will surmise that some two thousand years before
The blue sky was awash with colorless peacocks
And rising scholars will excavate superb fossils
From regions glittering with iced nitrogen
In the very upper reaches of the atmosphere
Or they might just stumble
Upon the giant footsteps of translucent man
In a stratified plane of Cretaceous sandstone

The propositions that you have before you are without exception
Asserted within the confines of a four-dimensional continuum
As the nature of the mental state and time in and of themselves

Miyazawa Kenji
20 January 1924

おそらくこれから二千年もたつたころは
それ相当のちがつた地質学が流用され
相当した証拠もまた次次過去から現出し
みんなは二千年ぐらゐ前には
青ぞらいつぱいの無色な孔雀が居たとおもひ
新進の大学士たちは気圏のいちばんの上層
きらびやかな氷窒素のあたりから
すてきな化石を発掘したり
あるいは白堊紀砂岩の層面に
透明な人類の巨大な足跡を
発見するかもしれません

すべてこれらの命題は
心象や時間それ自身の性質として
第四次延長のなかで主張されます

大正十三年一月廿日　　宮沢賢治

surmise　推測する、推察する
awash with...　〜でいっぱいで、〜であふれて
rising　「新進の」
superb　「すてきな」、素晴らしい、見事な
stumble　よろめく、つまづく
stratified　層状の
Cretaceous　「白堊紀」
propositions　「命題」
four-dimensional continuum　「第四次延長」。四次元連続体のことだが、宮沢賢治のいう「第四次延長」には時間軸だけでなく心象も含まれるという説もある

ロジャー・パルバース
Roger Pulvers

作家、劇作家、演出家、翻訳家、映画監督、東京工業大学名誉教授。1944年、ニューヨークで生まれる。カリフォルニア大学ロサンゼルス校、ハーバード大学大学院卒業。ベトナム戦争への反発からアメリカを離れ、ワルシャワ、パリに留学ののち、1967年に初来日し、京都産業大学、東京工業大学で教鞭をとる。現在はオーストラリア在住。日本に度々帰国している。

著書には、『星砂物語』（小説：講談社）、『ぼくがアメリカ人をやめたワケ』（大沢章子訳　集英社インターナショナル）、『驚くべき日本語』（早川敦子訳　集英社）など多数。

宮沢賢治の翻訳・研究者としても知られ、『英語で読む銀河鉄道の夜』（ちくま文庫）、『賢治から、あなたへ　世界はすべてつながっている』（森本奈理訳　集英社インターナショナル）などの著書多数。

宮沢賢治 原文英訳シリーズ 1
『銀河鉄道の夜』を英語で読む

2023年6月10日　第1版第1刷発行

英訳・解説：ロジャー・パルバース

編集協力：熊沢敏之、田中和也、大岩根麻衣

装丁：松本田鶴子

カバー画像イラスト：わたほこり_AdobeStock, jenteva_AdobeStock
本文イラスト：ルーシー・パルバース

発行人：坂本由子
発行所：コスモピア株式会社
　　　　〒151-0053　東京都渋谷区代々木4-36-4　MCビル2F
営業部：TEL: 03-5302-8378　email: mas@cosmopier.com
編集部：TEL: 03-5302-8379　email: editorial@cosmopier.com

https://www.cosmopier.com/（コスモピア公式ホームページ）
https://e-st.cosmopier.com/（コスモピアeステーション）
https://ebc.cosmopier.com/（子ども英語ブッククラブ）
印刷：シナノ印刷株式会社

本書へのご意見・ご感想をお聞かせください。

本書をお買い上げいただき、誠にありがとうございます。

今後の出版の参考にさせていただきたいので、ぜひ、ご意見・ご感想をお聞かせください。（PC またはスマートフォンで下記のアンケートフォームよりお願いいたします）

アンケートにご協力いただいた方の中から抽選で毎月 10 名の方に、コスモピア・オンラインショップ（https://www.cosmopier.net/）でお使いいただける 500 円のクーポンを差し上げます。（当選メールをもって発表にかえさせていただきます）

https://forms.gle/oN82tStgsiMfmrwD7